MW01126239

"At the heart of every organization is the workforce and ensuring its effectiveness is the responsibility of HR technology. By sharing her deep knowledge and significant experience in managing accelerated change, Stacey Harris has delivered an innovative and practical handbook about the technologies that move business forward every day."
Jeanne Achille, CEO, The Devon Group

"*Introduction to HR Technologies* is essential reading for professionals at all levels working in the HRIS arena as it covers every facet of the HR landscape including past, present and future. It is an easy read that provides practical advice and thought-provoking questions to help you assess your current environment and grow your company."
Alison Silvester, AVP IT Leader of S&D IT, The Hartford

"Finally, a book for leaders that can actually make your work life better. Stacey does an exceptional job capturing the intimate details of the ever-changing state of work, human resources and HR technology. She breaks down complexities and outdated thinking, challenges people to think about human resources and technology differently and tackles the intersection of work and life. Her thoughtfulness and care for bringing human resources and HR technology closer to the business is a welcomed approach for leaders everywhere."
Lisa Sterling, Chief Administrative and HR Officer, Evercommerce

"Technology's role in continuing to position HR as critical to business performance is crucial – this book does a great job in exploring the impact it has had in the past, and opportunities for the future. It gives you insights as an HR leader on how, and why, you need to think about technology as a key part of your plan. Important food for thought!"
Lisa Stafford, Professor of Management, Director of Graduate MS in Management program, Fairfield University

"I could not put it down. As I read through this book, my thought was that it cannot come fast enough. With Human Capital at the top of the pyramid, we need to unleash our HR department to deal with the new realities and get away from the PROCESS focus. Reskill and have this department laser-focused on building a high-performance workforce to increase business outcomes. This is such welcome news, and every progressive HR leader needs to rethink not only their role, but the team's role. This takes us to a reskilling/upskilling effort like we have never witnessed before."
Ron Thomas, Managing Director, Strategy Focused Group

"Whether you are on point to find the best fit technology solution or you are new to the field of HR, this book is the primer you need to go from 0–60 on HR Technology. Stacey Harris is a master at informing you without overwhelming you with extraneous detail. Along the way, you'll enjoy her real-world stories – always keeping the 'human' in HR Tech."
Leighanne Levensaler, EVP of Corporate Strategy, Workday & Co-Head, Workday Ventures

"This is the kind of book you keep on your desk with pages folded, binder cracked, coffee stains on the cover – well-worn from thumbing through it again and again. An essential reference guide for seasoned HR technologists and aspiring people operations professionals alike."
Kyle Lagunas, GM Global Talent Acquisition Lead

"As we are emerging from a tumultuous 18-month period of time where the need for real time insights about our employees has never been more critical, *Introduction to HR Technologies* provides HR and technology practitioners with the roadmap they need to fully understand their HR tech investments. Stacey Harris is a terrific writer and researcher who does a great job of laying out the strategic and practical realities of why HR technology matters now more than ever before, and how to leverage these solutions to achieve your performance and process objectives."
Kim Seals, Investor, Advisor, Board Member

Introduction to HR Technologies

Understand how to use technology to improve performance and processes

Stacey Harris

KoganPage

Publisher's note

Every possible effort has been made to ensure that the information contained in this book is accurate at the time of going to press, and the publishers and author cannot accept responsibility for any errors or omissions, however caused. No responsibility for loss or damage occasioned to any person acting, or refraining from action, as a result of the material in this publication can be accepted by the editor, the publisher or the author.

First published in Great Britain and the United States in 2021 by Kogan Page Limited

Apart from any fair dealing for the purposes of research or private study, or criticism or review, as permitted under the Copyright, Designs and Patents Act 1988, this publication may only be reproduced, stored or transmitted, in any form or by any means, with the prior permission in writing of the publishers, or in the case of reprographic reproduction in accordance with the terms and licences issued by the CLA. Enquiries concerning reproduction outside these terms should be sent to the publishers at the undermentioned addresses:

2nd Floor, 45 Gee Street
London EC1V 3RS
United Kingdom

www.koganpage.com

1518 Walnut Street, Suite 1100
Philadelphia PA 19102
USA

4737/23 Ansari Road
Daryaganj
New Delhi 110002
India

Kogan Page books are printed on paper from sustainable forests.

© Stacey Harris 2021

The right of Stacey Harris to be identified as the author of this work has been asserted by her in accordance with the Copyright, Designs and Patents Act 1988.

ISBNs

Hardback   9781789665291
Paperback   9781789665277
Ebook   9781789665284

British Library Cataloguing-in-Publication Data

A CIP record for this book is available from the British Library.

Library of Congress Control Number

2021939267

Typeset by Graphicraft Limited, Hong Kong
Printed and bound in India by Replika Press Pvt Ltd

For my husband Charles (Toby) and my best friend Edwina.
The two book ends of my life, gone too soon – but your stubborn
belief that I could always go further is why this book exists.
I love and miss you both.

CONTENTS

PREFACE

Work, me and the future

One of my earliest memories as a child was of visiting my father at work. I can remember sitting in the darkened aqua-green back seat of my parents 1970s' Chevy Impala, filled with excitement, jumping from shadow to light as we passed under the streetlamps that barely covered that end of town. As soon as my mother slowed down and I could hear the clanking of the big metal gates, I would scramble to my knees to look out the window in awe. This was in the days before car seats were required and curious children slid around vinyl back-seats with abandon. As I peeped over the edge of the door, hands flattened against the cold window, making outlines on the glass, my little heart would pound furiously as the car wound its way through a magical land. Mouth agape, I would take it all in slowly, from the large white towers as tall as city buildings rising all around us, to dark, oddly shaped dragons perched atop the highest peaks spewing fire and steam in every direction, to sparkling fairies floating in the air and gigantic metal monsters lining the road puffing smoke and growling furiously as they encroached on our little car. I wasn't quite four years old at this point in my life, and in my little world visiting my father at work meant we needed to travel to a faraway land, through the loud city, under mountains and over immense bridges to finally reach his side. I loved visiting my father at work – this foreign world so different from our little suburban home was filled with excitement and adventure, and in the centre of this fairy land was a warm yellow office, with metal desks and cushy chairs that my father would hoist me up on so that I could reach the top of the desk and often find a stray mint or butterscotch I could snatch from the desk.

In reality my father was a 24-hour on-call supervisor at a large petro-leum storage and distribution station that sat on the edge of Pittsburgh, Pennsylvania. My fairy land was made up of three-storey-high reserve towers that filled a major distribution centre that processed over 40,000 gallons of petroleum every night. My father's job was to measure the weight of the fluid coming through the pipes, making sure the right product was placed into the right tank. You probably did not know this, but a single pipeline is used to ship all kinds of petroleum around the US, including standard diesel and gasoline, and the operators at that time carefully watched the fluid weight to know when to shift the pipes from one reserve tank to another. They also managed a dangerous process called vapour recovery, where pipes were vented on a regular basis to release gas and fume build-up, a bad thing in a highly flammable area. The rare instances when we were able to visit him at work were usually due to plummeting winter temperatures that would require additional layers of clothing for my father, who spent his evenings climbing massive oil and gas tanks 40ft high, monitoring the level, mixture and fumes – ensuring the gas and diesel reached their final destination inside the city without incident. Until I was much older I never realized how dangerous and difficult that job must have been for my father, and although he was paid very well at the time for his expertise, he came home every morning dead tired and covered from head to toe in soot, with the smell of gas following him through the door – I can remember my mum telling my aunt that she had to wash his work clothing twice to get it clean and remove the smell of gas. In addition to working in a dangerous environment at all hours of the day, my father's job required him to be on constant standby for work, so that he missed school events, family picnics and holidays on a regular basis. The supervisor's role was so hard to fill and to train for that my father was required to move every two to three years to train up new teams and fill open positions. I spent years blaming my father for my lack of friends because we moved so often, when honestly I was just a bossy kid who spent most of my time inside a book – but I am sure my father was pained by my lack of gratitude and understanding.

When I was 12 years old, against everyone's recommendations my father quit the well-paying oil job and decided to become a teacher – completely changing our lives, and his, and teaching me my very first lesson on the importance of understanding your own capabilities and controlling your own destiny. I have no idea what that manager was thinking when my dad handed in his resignation in 1985, but I am sure it was not much different than any manager today who loses a highly skilled employee with no one ready to replace them: Damn!

Although I was never aware of it, the Human Resources (HR) policies and HR Technology that my parents interacted with throughout their careers had a major impact on my life as I was growing up. In my early years all my father's missed holidays were due to an HR work policy. The need for my family to move every two years, causing me to lose my pet parakeet and my mother to lose her finest china, was due to poor recruiting and work environments. The regular pay cheque that I remember my mother cashing every two weeks before she went grocery shopping and took us to Baskin Robbins 31 Flavors of Ice-Cream was made possible by a piece of early green-screen technology, where the earliest payroll administrators would receive hundreds of Manila envelopes with handwritten timesheets like my father's and spend hours typing the data into this new thing called a payroll system. When I was 15 and my mother took six months off work on family medical leave to take care of my grandmother, who was dying of cancer, it was made possible because of HR regulations, policies, labour contracts and technology.

As I entered the work world myself, the hidden world of HR and HR Technology was a silent part of almost every major event in my life. Somewhere in a scrapbook buried in a closet, I still have my first pay stub from my first job as a camp counsellor at the YMCA. I was so proud of that first pay packet – it was a total of $126 and it meant freedom. I can remember my first training video and onboarding programme that had me using an automated telephone exam when I got a waitressing job at 16 – the same restaurant where several years later I met my husband, a short-order cook, for the first time and finagled my schedule to make sure we were on the same shifts. As both my sons were born, I remember trying to figure out maternity leave options – the first job gave me a whole four weeks of unpaid leave for my eldest son and all the paperwork was manual, but by the time my second son came along I was filling out leave forms online and receiving a whopping six weeks' paid leave to spend with him. When I finished my graduate programme in Education and Instructional Technology, I'll never forget how exciting it was to complete my first online job application and mark that masters-level box in the hopes of moving my career forward for my little family. Just seven years later, I would find myself a part of the largest global recession and job-reduction practices in years, which led me to one of the most important work relationships of my career. Our organization offered outplacement services and technology, and there I met an outplacement counsellor who changed my life. She reminded me that I had skills and capabilities far beyond my current role, and she provided assessments and online resources to help me rediscover what I wanted to do with my life and where I wanted to be in the future – and, most importantly, she stopped me from taking the first job offer that came along, because she had seen the data and knew that I could do better. She convinced me to wait until I received a job offer from a budding research firm located in Oakland, California, which started me on my consulting and research career that is such a big part of my world today. Then in 2014, just after starting a new job focused on researching HR Technology environments, not long after I had used an online tool to select benefits that would become so critical to my family, my husband was diagnosed with terminal cancer. We lost him in 2016, and once again HR policies and technology played a major role in my world. I was given time off for my grieving and had to change my benefits programme to remove my husband. I had to figure out what forms required I now be marked as a widow and how many exemptions I now needed on my tax forms. I had to think about ways to provide more opportunities and better rewards for the team members who stepped up while I was battling my worst nightmare, and eventually I broke down and had to use the employee assistance programme to pick myself up off the ground and work again.

Work and our personal lives are not nearly as separated as we like to imagine in the corporate world, and Human Resources is the means by which these two worlds connect. Everything we do in HR and HR Technology has an impact on our business, our employees and ultimately their personal lives. Sometimes that impact is noble and good, but in other cases that impact can be dangerous and disheartening. In a world where the stories about the abuse of power and technology abound, it can be easy to become cynical about organizations in general, and specifically about the role of HR and HR Technology. There is another side to this story though, and for every bad actor there are hundreds of hard-working HR professionals and technologists doing good every day of the year. This book is specifically for those people, the ones trying to figure out how organizational goals can coincide with human goals, and how technology can be responsibly harnessed to reach a better future.

Someone once asked me why I do what I do. And much like my father who often said he became a teacher because it was just who he was – he was a teacher – I have often felt that I research and write about HR because that is just who I am – I am a researcher. I start every conversation with a question, even if the answer is not easy or pretty, even if the world does not always work the way I think it should. Much like that little girl who poked her head out, too curious to be scared, I am still in awe of the world I see around me; I find beauty in the chaos and believe that as human beings we can create our own fairy tales if we just have enough knowledge.

HR and HR Technology environments

Throughout history, the Human Resources function has fought a constant battle to balance its role as employee advocate, business leader and organizational culture keeper. The critical nature of each of these roles demands focus and attention, yet most HR professionals would say balancing these competing agendas puts them in a no-win situation. I spent my early years as an HR practitioner on the front lines of this battle – watching a multitude of savvy, hard-working HR leaders wage a constant up hill campaign for the respect this difficult position demands inside every organization.

For the past ten years I have spent my career researching what makes a great HR function, one that can balance competing agendas and achieve the desired outcomes. I started out looking for HR organizations that leveraged technology, processes and resources more effectively than anyone else and these were well-run HR functions, but they were often missing a critical focus on organizational outcomes. These organizations were often relegated to compliance-based HR functions.

So, I went looking for best practice HR organizations led by well-respected HR leaders, heading up major HR transformation efforts. These were exciting organizations to work with, they were focused on industry best practices and often working with the newest and coolest HR technologies. These organizations thought more about the employee experience, but often didn't align that with the reality of the organizational culture or business practices. It was a struggle for these organizations to maintain best practices on an ongoing basis without the business connections.

Finally, I started asking different questions, researching organizations that achieved outcomes in step with their culture and employees, rather than at their expense. I went looking for functions that embraced their role as both business leader and employee advocate in a way that their operational colleagues could no longer ignore. I went looking for organizations that said their HR Technology was being used to inform business decisions and enterprise strategies. What I found were amazing outcome-focused organizations that treated HR as their secret weapon – and leveraged HR practices and technology in ways that were unique to their organization's ability to achieve phenomenal achievements.

In the midst of this research, I realized that there was a fundamental issue with how organizations were leveraging their HR Technology. Most organizations, even the most forward-thinking ones, were using their individual HR Technology as a means to an end, leveraging it for the moment to accomplish a task or achieve a short-term outcome – but they weren't viewing it as a dynamic system. Outcome-focused organizations specifically looked at their HR Technology environments as interconnected and hopefully highly self-sufficient environments. These environments were filled with data, workflows and content more valuable in aggregate than in their individual pieces. A highly connected HR Technology environment allowed the organization to work more efficiently but also more thoughtfully – to value the individual employee as part of the whole organization.

One way to think about a highly connected HR Technology environment is to envision your local community – no matter where you live, your community has a mixture of government buildings, businesses and homes for personal use. In a community, every individual building is important and has a critical role to play, but its value increases or decreases based on the location and management of the community. Some buildings like the police station, fire station and courthouse have specific community-wide services that everyone uses from time to time, much like enterprise applications, while other buildings like businesses or homes service only a subset of the community and thus aren't central but are still valuable, like specific functional applications in marketing or operations. A community stays connected through many factors, for example the basics of water and electricity are important in most communities and require community standards like voltage and pressure levels, much like basic information sharing, such as primary employee IDs or security configurations that require standards at an enterprise level. Communities that are also connected through other services like news outlets or community groups can run more efficiently and make sure everyone is informed and updated on the latest community events, changes or needs. In a highly connected HR Technology environment, these would be your integration points for information passed back and forth to allow the organization to work more efficiently and with more overall knowledge. This analogy could be expanded in multiple ways, but hopefully you can see how treating your HR Technology more like a community than a commodity could garner greater overall outcomes.

The first step in understanding an HR Technology environment that works like a self-supporting community is to understand the basics of the current HR Technology industry. HR professionals are at the centre of this conversation. They needed to change HR at a fundamental level – and to do that they needed to understand the resources and technology available to them to help achieve this transition. This is the basis of this book, to provide a clear overview of the current HR Technology landscape. I will explore each individual application and how it fits into the broader community of HR

Technology applications. I'll look at the various technology audiences and implementation practices that make the greatest difference in outcomes, and share insights on where the market is heading and how emerging technologies will play a role in the future of HR. Along the way the book provides case studies and hands-on activities to help you gain personal knowledge of your own HR Technology landscape.

01

What is Human Resources Technology?

Introduction

Over 30 years ago HR Technology was in its infancy, just a kernel of an idea held by those industry leaders who understood the power of data and automation. Looking back with awe and amazement at the technical accomplishments of this industry, we are ever mindful that HR still exists as a very personal experience for the individual. On the corporate side, HR Technology provides the vehicle through which organizations streamline processes, effectively allocate resources and innovate within their HR function.

For the workforce, our personal lives have become more integrated with our work lives, illustrating the point that when HR Technology works at its best, it provides the framework through which balance can be achieved for everyone. Looking forward, HR Technology may be facing its greatest challenge yet – the future will not be judged by cost savings and ease of use but rather by value creation and workforce experiences. In this new world, transparency will be expected and yet trust is paramount – and the responsibility for enterprise communications may fall to tomorrow's HR Technology environments.

The definitions

Human Resources Technology is a broad term used to describe a system of software applications and the supporting hardware necessary to operate and automate the work of managing an organization's workforce. The breadth of technology included under the umbrella term 'Human Resources Technology' varies widely based on the span of responsibilities found in each Human Resources organization and how the term 'workforce' is defined for each organization.

Breaking this definition down even further, an organization's workforce or Human Resources is everyone that leads, manages and accomplishes the work of an organization who is compensated in some way for their efforts. The Human Resources function is a department within an organization that is responsible for overseeing the formal systems used to manage a workforce.

Historically, the HR function was primarily responsible for acquiring, paying and possibly developing employees. That definition is so narrow that it barely resembles the strategic mandate of today's HR organization. No matter the size or maturity of an HR function, we generally see that it is overseeing several critical practice areas that include:

- core HR administration;
- service delivery;
- time management;
- talent management;
- analytics and planning;
- emerging HR practices.

Each of these categories as viewed in Figure 1.1 has its own professional standards, strategies, processes, defined responsibilities, compliance requirements, workflows and data sets – and these will be discussed in detail later in the book. For exceedingly small organizations, those with fewer than 25 employees, many of these management tasks can be handled manually via spreadsheets or outsourced to service organizations. If a small organization is outsourcing the management of these processes, it might use an accounting firm, a professional employer organization (PEO) within the United States, or a global employment organization (GEO) outside the US; in all cases some form of technology is still being used to manage your workforce.

FIGURE 1.1   The HR application categories

As organizations grow in size and complexity, they eventually find it necessary to move away from manual workloads or service providers and begin the process of selecting, adopting and managing their own processes and the supporting HR Technology environments. There is no hard-and-fast rule concerning the timing of this transition, but there are a few business or organizational situations that often lead to the decision to begin purchasing HR Technology:

- diverse work environments, including a mixture of hourly, exempt and non-exempt workers;
- rapid expansion, leading to employees in multiple cities, states, provinces, countries or regions;
- rapid growth, leading to an increased volume of hiring and onboarding;
- rapid change, leading to greater need for learning or reskilling;
- cost concerns, leading to an increased focus on time, scheduling and performance management;
- tight talent markets, leading to greater need for contingent workers, workforce career management and benefit options.

In each of these cases, organizations are looking for new technology that will reduce administrative efforts and improve outcomes for end-users and ultimately the business. The technology selected depends on industry standards, market availability and the organization's selection process. An organization should look for a solution that fits culturally, achieves its strategic outcomes and will be able to integrate effectively into a current or future data governance model.

EXAMPLE

A rapidly growing organization that has sales goals dependent on well-trained customer support representatives is struggling to keep up with the hiring and onboarding demand of new employees. To achieve the desired outcome, the HR function has analysed the hiring and onboarding work and believes the best way to speed up the process is to automate some of the recruiting efforts, reduce the manual workload of managers inputting interview data and implement a self-service onboarding program for new employees. These process areas all fall under the talent management practice area. An HR function may look to acquire a point solution that just addresses the immediate hiring and onboarding needs, look at existing technology to see whether added modules could address the needs, or choose to think more broadly and select a full Talent Management suite that allows HR to address current and future needs. The selection process should focus on the outcome of growth, while taking into consideration that the organization has a culture of collaboration and management expects regular reporting from each function in a mobile format. These factors should emphasize a solution that can scale quickly, has team-based work environments and produces easily sharable, mobile-friendly reports.

The most common software applications developed to address these HR practice areas today are shown in Table 1.1.

Although this is an extensive list, it is not exhaustive. John Sumser, Chief Analyst for *HRExaminer* magazine, quotes in his book *The Birth of HR as a Systems Science* that there are over 100 discrete HR Technology application categories in the market.[1] I have selected the most common used in most HR organizations of an average size and complexity. These would be considered the building blocks of most HR Technology environments. The emerging HR practices are

TABLE 1.1 Most common software applications addressing HR practice areas

HR practice category	Common HR software applications
Core HR administration	• Payroll and tax administration • Human Resources management • Benefits administration • Health, safety and wellness
Service delivery	• Employee self-service • Manager self-service • Portals and workflow platforms • Helpdesk and case management • Engagement and feedback platforms • Content and communication platforms
Time management	• Time and attendance • Leave management • Absence management • Labour scheduling • Labour budgeting • Productivity/task management
Talent management	• Talent profile/skills management • Talent acquisition and recruiting • Onboarding and mobility • Learning and development • Performance management • Compensation and reward management • Succession and career planning
Analytics and planning	• HR and people analytics • HR data visualization • HR reporting and dashboards • HR data management and storage • Organizational planning and forecasting • Workforce planning and forecasting
Emerging HR practices	• Intelligent processes and insights • Data capturing and monitoring practices • Communication approaches • Workflow and work augmentation

constantly in development, including the use of social platforms, the Internet of Things and artificial intelligence, so this list is likely to grow and change over time.

A small warning when it comes to HR Technology vendors: we see hundreds of new HR Technology solutions enter the market every year, adding to an existing market of thousands of HR Technology vendors. Every solution provider feels they are fulfilling a unique gap in the industry and doing something totally different. In reality, most of them are offering overlapping solutions that only slightly innovate on existing applications. However, there is always hope for innovation, and generally there are 3–4 unique ideas a year that are worth watching for future application development.

Over the course of this book, we will be taking a closer look at each of these HR practice categories and their corresponding common HR software applications, along with details on who uses them, how they are selected and implemented, and what outcomes organizations achieve when these applications are fully utilized. We will also delve into the category of emerging technology and provide some guidance on how to include these applications into a solid, long-term HR Technology strategy.

Why you need to care

As a modern HR professional, you probably already live in a world inundated with technology – it is likely a part of your everyday life. You may wake up to the alarm on your phone, check the weather on your weather app or ask Alexa to read your morning emails. As technology is with you throughout the day, you generally do not think about where this data – be it the weather, news, emails or anything else – is coming from because you have configured and set up your personal technology. You know what parameters you gave it and what data it should be pulling to give you information and guidance. If you are not getting what you need from your personal technology, you make the effort to update your preferences, add applications or clear settings that are no longer relevant.

When we come to work it is just as easy to simply focus on the task at hand or the screen in front of us, forgetting that the underlying applications require the same level of careful setup and maintenance as our personal technology, but on a much larger scale to provide us with accurate and valuable insights.

HR applications are tools that enable us to achieve outcomes for HR, our organizations and the employees. Positive outcomes require that these tools are used by skilled HR professionals and educated workforces who understand the available resources and data they have at hand. Being informed of how the data is entered into the technology, and how interconnected or dependent one technology is on another, is helpful. Understanding the inherent logic and configured settings within HR applications is simply judicious. This type of knowledge gives you power and greater insight into the level of confidence you should have in the system's recommendations and what is required to achieve outcomes.

Although there are inherent struggles in trying to constantly navigate the shifting trends in HR technologies, it is worth the effort. HR professionals who effectively navigate their HR systems and available HR data make more informed decisions and are capable of more quickly weighing the opportunities and risks that come with either action or inaction. At the heart of our ever-changing work environments sits the workforce itself, people who are looking for opportunities to grow, develop and expand their future options. HR systems that embrace a more transparent and employee-driven work environment can make a difference. Organizations that are comfortable with their own strategy and internal culture can leverage HR Technology to cultivate an environment that supports their vision.

HANDS-ON ACTIVITIES

After each chapter I will provide recommended questions and activities to increase your personal HR Technology knowledge. This is an opportunity to start a conversation with your colleagues, mentors and leaders and to invest in your HR Technology journey.

- Does your company outsource employee services and employee technology to a PEO, GEO or accounting organization?
- Which of these HR service areas currently fall under the responsibility of your internal HR organization or an outsourced entity? (Mark these service areas as either Internal, External or Not Applicable.)

  o HR data management administration (Human Resource Management System or HRMS)

  o Payroll services

  o Benefit services

  o HR helpdesk/case management

  o HR communication

  o Health and safety reviews

  o Workforce time and attendance tracking

  o Leave request management

  o Workforce scheduling/project scheduling

  o Performance management process and services

  o Onboarding process and services

  o Recruiting process and services

  o Learning services process and services

  o HR and workforce reporting

  o Enterprise workforce planning

- Which of the HR applications in Table 1.2 are in use in your organization? (Mark them In Use, Implementing, Evaluating, Not Applicable/No Plans.)

TABLE 1.2

HR Practice Category	Common HR software applications
Core HR administration applications	• Payroll and tax administration • Human resource management • Benefits administration • Health, safety and wellness

(continued)

TABLE 1.2 (Continued)

HR Practice Category	Common HR software applications
Service delivery applications	• Employee self-service • Manager self-service • Portals and workflow platforms • Helpdesk and case management • Engagement and feedback platforms • Content and communication platforms
Time management applications	• Time and attendance • Leave management • Absence management • Labour scheduling • Labour budgeting • Productivity/task management
Talent management applications	• Talent profile/skills management • Talent acquisition and recruiting • Onboarding and mobility • Learning and development • Performance management • Compensation and reward management • Succession and career planning
Analytics and planning applications	• HR and people analytics platform • HR data visualization tool • HR reporting and dashboards • HR data management and storage • Organizational planning and forecasting • Workforce planning and forecasting
Emerging HR applications	• Intelligent processes and insights • Data capturing and monitoring practices • Communication approaches • Workflow and work augmentation

Endnote

1 *The 2020 Index of Intelligent Tools in HR Technology: The Birth of HR as a Systems Science. HRExaminer*, 2 October 2019

02

The history of HR Technology use

Introduction

My first big corporate job was at a large bank in north-east Ohio, where I was hired to work on a corporate training initiative for the retails bank division. I headed to the big city of Cleveland, Ohio and the thirty-first floor of the not quite tallest building in the city with mixed levels of excitement and fear on my first day. I was the youngest member of the team and I had just finished my master's degree focused on corporate learning. I worried about lots of things back then – would I fit in, would I know how to handle office politics, where the hell do you park in the city, would I get lost getting to my desk in the middle of the thirty-first floor, could you really tell the building was swaying by the swishing of the toilet bowls? But I never realized that the hardest part of my new job would be dealing with the corporate technology. I mean, I was fresh out of university, where I had been researching the hottest technology in the market. This was a huge organization with tons of resources, I just assumed I would have the coolest technology at my fingertips. Cue my gasp when I realized the email system I'd be using every day was a 10-year-old program called Lotus Notes and the most up-to-date learning technology they had at an enterprise level was a phone-based registrar system where employees called in to sign up for classroom training.

When I started asking about why newer technology was not on the horizon, the response was simple: we have just finished upgrading this email system to the tune of a $2 million investment and no one wants to undertake a new project right now. I quickly realized that if I was going to be taken seriously when I asked about new technology, I needed to know the history of my existing technology. I needed to understand how long an application had been in place, what the original investments were, the upgrade timelines, the vendor relationship – I needed to do more than just learn about the hot new technology, I needed to understand everything I could about the technology we already had. Although Lotus Notes was still in place long after I left that organization, I can proudly say that as I was leaving for another job, my investment in learning the existing systems and making the case for a new learning management system had them in evaluation mode as I was walking out the door.

As we noted earlier, technology, and HR Technology, is always evolving and innovating. A short detour to review the history of each of the topics discussed in this book is well worth your time as a reader. Organizations, much like communities, have unique cultures and histories, no matter their shared industry, location or even established dates. They are as different from each other as your personality is from that of your work colleagues. Cultures are the cumulative makeup of founding principles, past successes and failures, future expectations and the makeup of everyone that was previously hired. These unique cultures ensure that no two organizations will have the exact same approach to HR and thus will have different approaches to how and when they acquire HR Technology.

The definitions

Before we peer into the past and share a historical perspective of the HR Technology industry it is critical to understand a few foundational technology terms that will help clarify each major technical advancement we'll be discussing.

What is an HR Technology system made of?

- **Computer program** – a collection of data and instructions that can be executed by a computer to accomplish a specific result or perform a specific task.

- **Software application** – a program or group of programs designed for end-users.
- **Software module** – a part of a software program that creates a separate space or unit in a software application that may partition off data sets, security or content.
- **Application programming interface (API)** – a software intermediary or function that allows two applications to communicate with each other by creating guidelines for accessing data, external software components, operating systems or microservices.
- **Enterprise resource planning (ERP) application** – business management software application that includes a suite of integrated software modules necessary to manage an organization's business effort, including but not limited to finance, supply chain and Human Resource applications. These are highly configurable applications.
- **Functional suite application** – a functional set of software modules built on industry best practices, tied to a specific functional area, such as a talent management suite, learning management suite or time management suite.
- **Best-of-breed application** – a single software application developed to address a specific niche area of business practices; a more focused software application design to be the best or earliest in the industry over a broader integrated application suite.

How is HR Technology purchased?

HR Technology is purchased in two main ways in today's business environments: perpetual licensed software and subscription software.

Perpetual licensed software is when an organization purchases a full licence and owns the software, allowing it to install the software in its own (on-premise) local server environment or in a hosted environment. The purchaser is responsible for installing, maintaining, securing and backing up the application and its data. End-users access the application via a company network for as long as the software continues to be viable.

Subscription software (software as a service or SaaS) is when an organization purchases per-user, subscription-level access to the software and it resides on the vendor's hardware – the vendor is responsible for system updates, maintenance and data backups. End-users access the application via internet access (cloud).

Where are the actual HR Technology systems housed?

- **Mainframe environment** – an early computer format, designed for high-volume, processor-intensive computing. Initially used only by the largest of organizations as the central processing unit and main memory for thin clients (non-processing computers). The earliest HR applications were housed in these environments.

- **Client-server application model** – a distributed structure that partitioned programs and workloads between back-office servers and desktop clients. The desktop clients ran the applications but requested centralized data and information from the remote servers.

- **Public cloud environment (infrastructure as a service or IaaS)** – a type of on-demand computing environment that makes resources/ applications and data available via public internet like Amazon Web Services (AWS) or Microsoft Azure. It is highly scalable and allows for regional data locations and multiple redundancies.

- **Single tenancy** – a single instance of a software application and supporting infrastructure that houses a single customer's data. In a cloud environment, vendors maintain a standard code that is duplicated for everyone, but a customer's individual instance and data are housed separately from those of every other client. This environment allows for minor customization.

- **Multi-tenancy** – an environment where multiple clients share a single infrastructure and single set of code and may even share databases. In this environment customers share resources, reducing cost and security issues, and separate their personal instance virtually. This environment allows for no customization, only configuration.

The technology timelines

Over the lifetime of your career, it is likely that you will work for organizations that always purchase the newest technologies as well as those that will hold on to legacy applications long after their support dates have expired, and everyone in between. A basic awareness of computer and software history will help give context for the more granular history we will be discussing for the HR industry. As an HR professional, understanding these historical details and how the HR Technology industry has developed over the past several decades will better equip you to understand the possibilities and limitations of your current HR Technology environment and set you up for a more informed decision on possible improvements in your own HR Technology environment.

1980s–1990s: Work has the best toys

In the 1980s and 1990s the idea of a personal computer system was just emerging and until the internet came about most people's primary interaction with a personal computer was in their work environment. In 1983 my dad took a second job working at an Apple retail store and bought an Apple IIe. We were the first kids on the block to have our own personal computer, with a stack of floppy disks that played games like 'Cranston Manor', 'Oregon Trail' and 'Asteroids'. When you started the computer, it was just a blinking green square at the bottom of the screen, and until you put in a disk and entered the right programming words, nothing happened. Still, for a period of about two years, our house was the coolest house on the block. User expectations for any technology were low.

Below are a few key technology events that were examples of this decade's technology evolution:

- 1975: the first personal computer was introduced as a build-it-yourself kit, the Altair 8800.
- 1977: Apple launches Apple II – the first personal computer with a colour monitor and floppy drive.

- 1981: IBM PC launches MS-DOS operating system, expansion slots, floppy drives and monochrome displays.
- 1985: Microsoft releases Windows, a graphical user interface for PCs.
- 1989: Microsoft launches the Microsoft Office (bundling Excel, PowerPoint and Word).

HR TECHNOLOGY HISTORY

1980s–1990s: Rise of client-server networks

Over 30 years ago, the emerging HR Technology market had few standard applications to purchase off the shelf, leaving organizations to design and build a plethora of in-house applications. In addition to limited overall options, only the biggest organizations could afford or were expected to have enterprise business software – so HR applications were designed specifically for these large, often global, organizations with a full staff of existing HR and IT administrators as their primary audience. In these environments, HR Technology evolved to focus on HR process management and administration. In the earliest days, these applications ran on mainframe computers, but throughout the late 1980s into the early 1990s these were being slowly replaced by client-server environments and ran on in-house servers with local networked desktop users. Although they were initially purchased as off-the-shelf applications, they were highly customized for each business unit and very few people inside an organization had access to these applications beyond the administration roles. In most cases these were Human Resources information systems (HRIS), payroll or time tracking applications purchased as an extension of the existing ERP business applications, or as part of outsourcing or service packages. These applications added little visible value to the lives of employees and business leaders but brought a huge amount of efficiency for the Human Resources function.

Here are a few key solution provider and vendor events that were examples of this decade's HR Technology evolution:

- 1983: Paychex HRMS (Human Resources management system), payroll and benefits outsourcing services go public.

- 1985: Kronos delivers first PC-based time and attendance application.
- 1986: SAP R/2 mainframe ERP launches early Human Resources management module.
- 1987: Kenexa Recruitment Services founded.
- 1989: PeopleSoft client-server HRMS application suite launches.

1990s–2000s: Rise of 24/7 internet access

In the early 1990s with the onset of graphical user interfaces in personal computers and the rise of the internet, end-user expectations changed – demand grew steadily for more visuals, content and access. Still, work was the place where you could get faster internet speed and in many cases information technology (IT) professionals had not yet caught up to the security risks inherent in downloading content from the internet. Much like today's younger workers, our generation took to AOL instant messaging like ducks to water, mixing discussions on lunch plans, office gossip and project work in ways that our more mature colleagues simply did not understand. At work we were introduced to new graphic-editing packages, word-processing tools and powerful multimedia tools like PowerPoint. End-users were experiencing cool multimedia interfaces on the internet built in new tools like Macromedia Flash, but these were tightly controlled environments viewed in media players, with proprietary technology. Everything on the internet was new and exciting, and filled with security issues we didn't understand as of yet.

Below are a few key technology events that were examples of this decade's technology evolution:

- 1991: America Online internet service relaunches.
- 1995: Amazon launches as an online bookseller.
- 1996: Adobe (Macromedia) launches Flash multimedia software for custom application development.
- 1998: Google launches as one of many internet search engines of its time.

- 1999: Alibaba launches its business-to-business, international, internet-based selling platform.
- 1999: Salesforce.com launches one of the first cloud-based business applications for sales automation.

HR TECHNOLOGY HISTORY

1990s–2000s: 24/7 internet access

In Human Resources with the onset of the internet, organizations were pushing hard to reduce manual HR processes and costly paperwork – and one way to accomplish this was to provide employees with direct access to the enterprise applications through service delivery tools, called employee and manager self-service. Finally, managers and employees could enter their own personal information, view direct reports, create schedules or enter time worked. This was one of the first enterprise applications to face the challenge of creating careful security standards, authorization requirements, and user experiences that were tailored for the broader employee population and accessible 24/7 via an external channel on the internet. Suddenly, hundreds of best-of-breed points solution applications hit the market focused on specific manager and employee HR use cases – such as scheduling, performance management, learning, recruiting – all leveraging this new expansive world of the internet. Large enterprise technology vendors were now competing with smaller, more nimble organizations, creating flashier and more accessible technology that needed to co-exist with their applications. Still, this was a big-company game, requiring access to servers, IT staff and now programmers to integrate multiple applications.

Here is an outline of a few key solution provider and vendor events that were examples of this decade's HR Technology evolution:

- 1990: Paycor, PC-based payroll processor, is founded for small and medium businesses.
- 1992: SAP R/3 client-server ERP launches, with a unique human resources management module.
- 1993: Lawson launches client-server ERP with finance, HR and supply chain modules.

- 1993: Ultimate Software launches UltiPro client-server human resource management and payroll.
- 1994: The Monster Board (TMB) launches, creating one of the first job-searching websites.
- 1997: Saba Software launches a stand-alone client-server learning management system (LMS).
- 1998: Skillsoft launches as an internet-based eLearning content provider.
- 1998: Paycom launches as an online payroll service provider for small and medium businesses.
- 1998: ADP launches Pay eXpert, one of the first complete payroll processing services for small and medium businesses.

2000s–2010: Rise of constant access and open source

With the onset of cloud-based technology in the early 2000s, every category of consumer and business application was disrupted with new serverless software, designed at lightning speed, accessible via the web and focused on providing consumer-friendly user environments. Much of this new technology was being developed with open source tools and was focused on breaking out of the executable boxes of the past generation's media players or static webpages. These were applications that were built based on data and interconnectedness and focused on speed and agility. Big businesses were starting to lose ground as the place to get access to the coolest tools and software. Now we were democratizing development and access, and end-users were beginning to realize that their personal technology environments were simply faster and more personalized than their work environments. Then we saw the rise of the mobile smart phone, which changed everything.

Below are a few key technology events that were examples of this decade's technology evolution:

- 2002: Blackberry launches its first 'mobile' phone.
- 2003: LinkedIn launches as a free and paid professional network.

- 2004: Facebook launches as the newest social networking platform.
- 2005: YouTube launches as a platform for uploading, sharing and searching video content.
- 2006: AWS launches as a public internet cloud option.
- 2006: MuleSoft launches as a cloud-based integration platform providing standard APIs across the tech market.
- 2006: Twitter, the micro-communication social networking platform tool, launches.
- 2007: Apple launches its first iteration of the iPhone.
- 2007: Netflix introduces streaming video content services.
- 2008: Roku launches one of the first streaming content players.
- 2010: Instagram launches its photograph-sharing social networking platform.

HR TECHNOLOGY HISTORY

2000s–2010: Everyone is moving to the cloud

In the early 2000s Human Resources organizations were struggling to manage end-user expectations and business requirements for internal systems – and everything was being disrupted by cloud applications and the desire for immediate access to data. Everyone had access to these applications, from the smallest organization to the largest, and although many of these applications started out as internet-based, with single installations for each client, over time most of them worked to transition their applications into true multi-tenant cloud applications that ensured all their customer environments could be maintained, updated and monitored all at once, which was more cost effective and efficient for the system vendors. In addition, the aggregate data that each customer brought to the table was becoming increasingly valuable in understanding the usage and best practices that could be garnered from the data. This environment made it easier than ever to develop cloud-based suites and niche HR applications, focused on unique cultural and strategic HR goals, including HR suites, talent suites, employee portals, candidate management, compensation and rewards.

Below are a few key solution provider and vendor events that were examples of this decade of HR Technology evolution:

- 2000: ADP launches Enterprise Payroll Services, web-based payroll and accounting platform for multinational organizations.
- 2001: SuccessFactors launches first cloud-based performance management module.
- 2002: Ultimate Software relaunches UltiPro as a multi-tenant cloud platform.
- 2003: LinkedIn launches as a free and paid professional network, expanding over time to a job board and recruiter sourcing site.
- 2004: SumTotal Systems forms (from Click2learn/Docent) as a cloud-based talent suite with learning, performance and career modules.
- 2004: Taleo forms (from ViaSite/Recruitsoft) as a cloud-based applicant-tracking system, then expanded to a talent suite.
- 2004: Oracle announces acquisition of PeopleSoft.
- 2005: Cornerstone OnDemand relaunches as a cloud-based talent management suite, with learning, performance and career modules.
- 2005: Kenexa acquires BrassRing and relaunches as a talent suite, with applicant tracking, candidate searching and performance management.
- 2006: Workday launches first version of its cloud-based Workday Human Capital Management application.
- 2008: Glassdoor launches as a company-review website, expanding over time to a job board site for recruiters.

2010–2020: Mobile first and consumer friendly

In the last decade end-users have been completely monopolized by the connection to their personal devices: phones, tablets, wearables. The expectations for the level of personalization and ease of use have become so high that businesses have given up trying to control everything and over 70 per cent of organizations in Sapient Insights' 2019–2020 annual HR Systems Survey had some form of a 'bring your own device' standard to allow employees to use their own devices in their work environments and to access work applications.

A mobile-first world created users that expected applications to provide more than just a place to enter or access data, but also to offer business recommendations, reminders, insights, community connections and best practices, all at their fingertips, just like their personal applications do for their health, home security or music applications.

Below are a few key technology events that were examples of this decade's technology evolution:

- 2011: Uber launches its ridesharing app as a new gig economy for sharing resources.
- 2011: Microsoft launches Office 365 as the newest model of subscription application buying.
- 2012: Oculus VR launches its first virtual reality headset.
- 2012: Slack team collaboration and messaging application launches.
- 2014: Amazon launches its first smart speaker and assistant in an 'Echo'.
- 2015: Apple launches its first wearable smartwatch.
- 2017: TikTok (Douyin), a China-based video-sharing social networking service, rises to prominence.
- 2019: SAP purchases Qualtrics, a survey and experience management platform.

HR TECHNOLOGY HISTORY

2010–2020: The consumerization of HR Tech

In the last decade through a slew of acquisitions and increased competition, the HR Technology market became highly commoditized, with similar off-the-shelf product offerings from vendor to vendor and increased competition from consumer- and IT-focused vendors such as Google, Microsoft and ServiceNow. Today almost every aspect of HR has been digitized into application areas and offered as purchasable modules, often now in public cloud environments such as Amazon Web Services, Azure or Google Cloud. Today organizations could buy entire ERP and HR suites that meet 80 per cent of their organizational HR needs out of the box and search pre-approved marketplaces and partner lists for the remaining 20 per cent of the applications they feel need to be unique to their organization. The current focus for most HR Technology vendors is on increasing market share by offering faster services, at cheaper prices, while matching specific buyers' needs through artificial intelligence, personalization and matching cultural expectations. For HR Technology buyers this decade was all about trying to manage and integrate multiple applications while trying to increase adoption of applications with better user experiences and keep the growing data sets clean enough for company decision making.

Below are a few key solution provider and vendor events that were examples of this decade's HR Technology evolution:

- 2011: Oracle releases first version of cloud-based Fusion ERP applications, including Human Resources.
- 2011: Infor multi-system conglomerate acquires Lawson ERP/HR focused on the healthcare industry.
- 2011: ADP payroll service provider and small business payroll software provider launches cloud-based HCM Vantage, HR, payroll, and talent suite for organizations with more than 1,000 employees.
- 2012: Ceridian acquires cloud HR, payroll and time management application Dayforce.
- 2012: IBM acquires Kenexa (BrassRing) and builds out Watson AI-powered HR and talent platform.
- 2012: Oracle acquires Taleo and rebrands Fusion HR to HCM Cloud.
- 2012: SAP acquires SuccessFactors and rebrands as SuccessFactors Employee Central.
- 2014: Skillsoft acquires SumTotal Systems and becomes a talent management option.
- 2016: Microsoft acquires LinkedIn and changes the dynamics about who owns the data.
- 2017: ServiceNow IT Help Desk application launches HR Service Delivery module.

- 2019: ADP launches a public cloud HCM application, based on team management, Next Gen HCM.
- 2020: Ultimate Software and Kronos Software merge to form Ultimate Kronos Group (UKG).
- 2021 Microsoft launches Viva, an employee experience platform.

Special note on 2020 and how it changed our world

In 2020 we faced a global pandemic, known generally as COVID-19, followed swiftly by a worldwide economic slowdown as countries around the globe focused inwards, closed borders, mandated stay-at-home orders and desperately tried to stop the spread of this deadly disease. The business world shook, and for the largest and most global companies, the early part of 2020 was a rapid rush to get employees home and in safe locations. For the smallest companies, their day-to-day existence was based on their industry, location and ability to shift business models.

We shared an experience of overwhelming loss due to COVID-19, a breaking point in social justice movements and economic uncertainties that washed across the globe. In the midst of these challenges, we also saw natural disasters, political upheavals and widespread mental health issues brought on by continuous loss and isolation. In this environment, it was never more important for the Human Resources function to balance the needs of both the organization and the employees. Literally overnight, HR functions were asked to reimagine the work environment and make ongoing critical decisions about the safety and sustainability of the workplace. The importance of HR Technology took on a completely new meaning in 2020.

The business of HR is always about achieving outcomes – how we do so makes all the difference. 2020 brought into sharp focus just how diverse we are when it comes to achieving business outcomes and meeting the needs of our employees. We also saw huge shifts by industry: healthcare and grocery stores saw rapidly increasing workloads for front-line employees, while travel and entertainment industries furloughed thousands of field employees overnight as businesses closed for undetermined amounts of time. Some organizations managed the crisis by focusing only on the bottom line, choosing to keep workers in possibly unsafe environments or rushing layoffs without proper communications. Other organizations chose to gather data, focus on safety, make leadership-level sacrifices, have clear communication during workforce reductions, and innovate and change where possible. The No. 1 response to the COVID-19 crisis, in almost every industry and region, was redistribution of an organization's critical workforce – making the work of HR a key factor in overall survival.[1]

Although overall HR Technology spending was decreasing, organizations were investing heavily in areas needed to support shifting work demands and manage safe work environments. The top initiatives HR organizations undertook in 2020 included:

- increasing remote work options and capabilities;
- implementing COVID-19 employee tracking, tracing and assessment tools;
- implementing new communications processes and technology;
- creating more flexible compensation models, allowing for bonuses, pay decreases and hybrid pay models;
- creating pod-based work schedules and new team working environments to ensure critical workforces were protected;
- implementing policies, technology and models for distanced and safe work environments;
- implementing new social responsibility standards, metrics and governance models.

Many of these initiatives started as part of how organizations were addressing the healthcare crisis, but it's likely they will continue to expand or combine these efforts with their active work on social justice efforts and future expectations for how the company will continue to work.

FIGURE 2.1 Percentage of organizations with 50 per cent or more remote workers, 2020

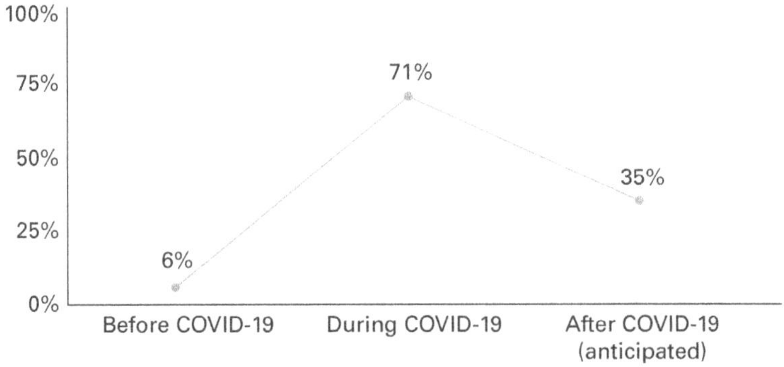

SOURCE   Sapient Insights, 2020–2021 HR Systems Survey White Paper, 23rd Annual Edition

For example, as seen in Figure 2.1, just 6 per cent of organizations said that 50 per cent or more of their workforce could work remotely prior to COVID-19; as our world quickly learned, organizations were able to ramp up work-from-home efforts in record time, with 71 per cent eventually having 50 per cent or more of their workforce working from a remote or home location. The more interesting fact is that 35 per cent of organizations stated that they expected to still have 50 per cent or more of their workforce working remotely after COVID-19, and expectations were similar across all industries. We expect 2020 will do more to reshape our work environments than any other year in the last quarter century. Heavy investments were made in biotechnology, health and safety, mental awareness and artificial intelligence throughout the year. It also forced critical conversations about systemic social injustices, biased algorithms, data privacy standards, ethical use of employee and consumer data, and the real value of various work requirements versus health and wellness.

Why you need to care

It is easy to think that looking forward should be the most important focus of your career, but you really have to understand what came before to understand where you truly are at the moment. The history of all the technology and businesses that came before is not only interesting to know, it is important to understand as the building block of today's existing systems. Data sets built in the 1980s, 1990s or 2000s will have biases built in, technology designed to support large business will have a harder time scaling to the needs of small businesses, and environments designed for use in offices are unlikely to consider the security risks inherent in a work-from-home work-force. It does not mean that any of these applications shouldn't be used, it simply means that as the HR professional advocating for their adoption or supporting their implementation, you need to be aware of the risks and add extra time for security analysis, configuration efforts or data cleaning to get the outcomes your organization needs.

HANDS-ON ACTIVITIES

- Identify the five oldest applications implemented in your HR Technology environment and note their launch dates and last update or upgrade dates.

- Identify the two newest applications in your HR Technology environment and note their launch dates and when they are due for an update or upgrade.

- Identify your organization's payroll application and its vendor. Look up the history of that vendor. Note any information you can find on important changes in ownership and major new product lines.

Endnote

1 Sapient Insights, 2020–2021 HR Systems Survey, 23rd Annual Edition

03

Who uses HR Technology?

Introduction

Knowing your audience is always important, and even more so when you are making major decisions about the technology they will be using every day. Early on in my career, I had the great opportunity to complete an internship at a large financial organization under the watchful eye of an amazing learning manager who took me under her wing and showed me the ropes well enough to ensure that I later got a full-time position with the organization. A few weeks into my internship, I learned the hard way one of my first lessons on knowing your audience.

I was working on a project for my learning manager that required information from a VP in another part of the organization, so I simply emailed the VP directly with the questions I had on the project and went on with my work. Later that day, my manager came to me with an email she had received from the VP enquiring as to why I was directly emailing him and asking for such sensitive employee information. I was too new to realize at the time that the employee training records and competency assessments I was asking about also included personal information on the employees. Although that was an important lesson on personal information for me to learn, the bigger issue had been my method and approach in communicating with someone at that level of the organization. There were procedures I later learned for requesting data and reports that could be anonymized, and if I had taken the time to learn the HR organization chart as my boss had recommended, I would have seen that there was a position reporting to this VP who had the role of data manager and oversaw these requests. These were important lessons for me on knowing my audience, but also on the importance of data security roles, data privacy and starting at the beginning of the process instead of rushing to the end.

The definitions

Today almost everyone inside an organization uses HR Technology in one form or another. From entering their personal information when getting hired to filling out time and attendance information or accessing payroll information, employees are probably using some form of an HR Technology application. HR professionals are no exception, and HR Technology is inextricably tied to the everyday tasks required of today's HR organization. An application user or persona is a specific person or role that uses the application to accomplish a task. In almost all business applications you have at least two types of users: end-users and administrators. End-users are really everyone that uses the technology to accomplish a specific task that is personal to them individually, or for their own job role or functional role within the organization. They are not completing the task on behalf of someone else. Technology administrators are end-users that are given additional permissions inside the application that allow them to maintain the permissions and security of other end-users within the system. They may also be tasked with configuring and maintaining the business application workflows, interface setup and reports. More technical administrators may also handle implementations, upgrades, integrations and vendor contracts. Before the advent of manager and employee self-service screens they also were the primary conduit between the business and the application, entering data, running reports and changing incorrect information. Even with manager and employee self-service, administrators still perform many of these tasks for organizations today.

As you can see, these roles do overlap, and in larger organizations they have different levels of personas in each category, but it is helpful to understand all the various personas that interact with an organization's HR Technology environment on a regular basis. Defining these different personas provides a basis for your required security configurations, various system use cases and your user experience requirements.

Another way to define your HR Technology personas is to create a matrix that outlines the various roles within your organization and the specific screens they would need to access within an application. Table 3.1 is just one example of how a matrix like this might look in a medium-sized organization.

TABLE 3.1   An example persona matrix for a medium-sized organization

	System setup	Security setup	Functional reporting	Business reporting	Team profile	Individual profile	Personal information
HRIT professional	X	X	X	X	X	X	
HRIT administrator	X	X	X	X	X	X	
HR functional admin			X	X	X	X	
HR helpdesk						X	
HR leadership			X	X	X	X	
HR business partner				X	X	X	
HR generalist			X		X	X	
Payroll administrator			X	X		X	
Benefits administrator			X	X		X	
Time and labour admin			X	X		X	
Recruiting professional			X				
Learning professional			X				
Compensation analyst			X				

(continued)

TABLE 3.1 (Continued)

HR analytics/ planning	X	X	X	X	
CEO	X	X	X		
Business leader		X	X		
Manager			X	X	
Employee				X	X
Temporary worker					X

For each persona within your organization, you will also want to capture specific demographics concerning where and when they might access the applications and any limitations they may have in accessing the applications in a standard format. For example, 20 per cent of managers may be in the corporate office with direct access to a desktop at all times, while 80 per cent may be field managers with limited desk access. Over 90 per cent may have access to smartphones and be willing to predominantly access the application through the phone. You will still need to provide desktop access for the 10 per cent without smartphones which is accessible via their home offices.

Understanding your user personas or roles is a first critical step in HR Technology selection and configuration, but eventually, as you gather more data and implement more sophisticated HR Technology environments, you will begin to cultivate a wealth of available data on your individual end-users that can be used to provide a more personalized experience for each end-user. The huge shift to work-from-home and distributed work environments precipitated by the COVID-19 pandemic is a prime example of how important it is to understand the personal work environments of our end-users.

The biggest change in tomorrow's workforce will be the expectation that organizations and institutions see every employee as individuals and value their individuality. Included in that expectation of individuality is how and when they interact with technology. The explosive focus on individuality is being driven, in part, by the fact that today's consumer technology has created an environment where our individual needs can be and are being met. We have personalized radio stations, regionalized automobiles, tailored marketing campaigns and local food challenges. Even in cultures and communities where the idea of individualism is less celebrated, we see technology that helps elevate individual ideas and voices without focusing on the person. Technologies that allow for crowdsourcing, sharing sites and even simple likes and dislikes provide both a voice and tremendous power to individuals.

Why you need to care

When people discuss the need to prepare for our changing workforce, it is easy to simplify the conversation down to a few characteristics that can be addressed with a defined set of best practices. We focus on a younger workforce or an older workforce. We think in terms of a more technology-savvy workforce or one that is more culturally separated. The reality is that tomorrow's workforce will simply be more diverse in all ways – and very aware of what makes them unique. In the last generation our workforce was generally focused on finding ways to fit the required mould for being successful; the desire to follow a defined plan for the path to success crossed borders, industries and generations. Organizations had comfortable prescribed plans and ways in which everyone worked in their environments, and for most of their employee and leadership roles they had a general formula for success that would work regardless of the location or industry. Tomorrow's workforce assumes that these technical advances that tailor to their individualism outside work will also be leveraged inside work.

As organizations grow and their workforces become more complex, capturing and making sense of individual workforce data requires planning. All HR technologies are designed to gather data effectively, but to meet the needs of our changing workforce they also need to be able to analyze that data, provide context and understanding, and present end-users with an experience that is unique to them.

As you develop a full picture of your HR Technology end-users, you will eventually need to understand much more to provide personalized experiences:

- regionally approved demographic information;
- current reporting structure;
- current work team environment;
- education experience;
- work experience;
- skills and capabilities;
- personal and professional goals;
- regional and cultural experiences;
- communication preferences;
- technology preferences;
- leadership preferences;
- work-related stressors.

Each data point is valuable, but it is the total profile that provides the greatest insight when thinking about HR Technology users of the future.

EXAMPLE

We know that the millennials and now Gen Zs are constant topics of conversation, and that they seem 'different' in a way that needs explanation. However, it is important to ask additional questions, such as how factors such as skills, education or geography play a part in our own generational bias. The Asia-Pacific market is well known to have one of the youngest and fastest growing workforces in the world, along with rapidly growing consumer markets and an emerging middle class with higher levels of spending power than ever before.[1] All these factors make the Asia-Pacific region an extremely attractive market for expansion, outsourcing and manufacturing, and organizations in these regions are beginning to invest in HR Technology to manage these large workforces.

A research effort on global workforces conducted by Sierra-Cedar[2] in 2018 found that although millennials overall were more likely to use employee and manager self-service tools to accomplish HR and personal tasks than any other generation, millennials in the Asia-Pacific offices were more likely to contact their HR department or their direct manager to complete HR administrative activities than those employees located in Europe or the United States. For example, only 2 per cent of European employees and 4 per cent of US employees predominantly contact their HR representative or direct manager to complete their performance reviews. In comparison, 10 per cent of Asia-Pacific employees contact an HR representative or a direct manager regularly to perform these tasks. Regional expectations and cultural standards can play a major role in the adoption of HR Technology.

As we are looking at personalization it is also important to understand our own biases versus actual data we can obtain from our workforce concerning their expectations or needs. If overall Asia-Pacific seems to be more likely to contact an HR representative or direct manager when completing an HR administrative task online, we wondered whether this also varied by age. One 'truism' about older workers is that they are less tech-savvy than younger workers, but even if this is true for writing code or social media skills, is this true when looking at employee self-service?

Not at all! In almost every area both in the aggregate data set and for the Asia-Pacific workforce alone respondents over the age of 30 were more likely to complete tasks online rather than contact their HR representative or direct manager. Please note that this data doesn't make any judgements on whether or not the managers are effective regardless of their age – an article from Harvard Business Review found that in a survey of 17,000 worldwide leaders, the average age of supervisors was 33 and the typical individual became a supervisor around the age of 30, today's millennial generation.[3] This research also found that on average individuals did not receive any leadership training until age 42 – 10 years after the individual began to supervise others. Organizations that move employees into management roles early are likely to find that these new first-level managers require more direct support from their HR representatives or their direct managers – and adjustments may need to be made to the expectations for HR systems manager self-service adoption levels. This data emphasizes the importance of gathering multiple levels of data and ensuring that information is placed in context before an organization makes enterprise-wide HR Technology decisions that may impact the individuals within their workforce. Assuming that a younger workforce, or younger managers, prefer online interactions and require less individual support could very well create an employee relations nightmare. Meanwhile, assuming that older employees are unwilling or unable to leverage HR manager self-service tools could be limiting your organization unnecessarily.

Increasing adoption and the investment your organization has placed in both time and resources in implementing any technology, but particularly HR Technology, requires a clear understanding of your end-users' needs, motivations and expectations. Without these you risk at best little to no use of the application, and at worst a system that is used to game the environment and push outcomes that are poor for employees and the organization.

HANDS-ON ACTIVITIES

- Obtain or create an organizational chart similar to the one in Table 3.2 for your payroll, HRMS and recruiting applications (if you are using these applications).

- Identify whether there is an HR or non-HR system that holds this information about you for the organization:

  ○ Regionally approved demographic information

  ○ Current reporting structure

  ○ Current work team environment

  ○ Education experience

  ○ Work experience

  ○ Skills and capabilities

  ○ Personal and professional goals

- o Regional and cultural experiences
- o Communication preferences
- o Technology preferences
- o Leadership preferences
- o Work-related stressors

TABLE 3.2

	System setup	Security setup	Functional reporting	Business reporting	Team profile	Individual profile	Personal information
HRIT professional							
HRIT administrator							
HR functional admin							
HR helpdesk							
HR leadership							
HR business partner							
HR generalist							
Payroll administrator							
Benefits administrator							
Time and labour admin							
Recruiting professional							
Learning professional							
Compensation analyst							
HR analytics/ planning							
CEO							

(continued)

TABLE 3.2 (Continued)

Business leader
Manager
Employee
Temporary worker
Other

Endnotes

1 Bourque, A (2014) Is your business ready for the world's emerging middle class? *Huff Post* https://www.huffpost.com/entry/is-your-business-ready-fo_b_6376056 (archived at https://perma.cc/ZHD4-6H5K)

2 Sierra-Cedar 2018 Employee Perspectives HR Technology Report

3 Zenger, J (2012) We wait too long to train our leaders, *Harvard Business Review*, https://hbr.org/2012/12/why-do-we-wait-so-long-to-trai (archived at https://perma.cc/H3D4-KRJ5)

04

Who owns HR Technology?

Introduction

At 15 I thought I knew everything there was to know about the work world. I mean, I had spent the last two years working as a camp counsellor for the YMCA down the road from my home – and I had figured out how to apply for the job all on my own, get myself to work every day, cashed my pay cheques, I even wrote my own end-of-year performance review. Really, what more could there be to the working world? I just did not understand why my parents thought it was so hard. My second foray into the work world would soon teach me that I knew extraordinarily little about listening, understanding roles and responsibilities, and the importance of knowing your real customer. I understood so little that I was fired about six months into my new job as the café waitress and cook at the local bowling alley in my hometown.

My new roles seemed pretty simple to me: take the orders, cook the café food and serve the customers. Well, I was 15 and punctuality was not a strong suit, nor was paying attention to my responsibilities. I made a point of always calling if I was going to be late, and my colleague never seemed to be upset so I did not see the issue, and yes, I was a little slow serving the bowling alley patrons, but I was taking the time to really get to know the customers who came into the café area to chat with me and they seemed to love me, and yes, the ketchup bottles were all supposed to be filled each night, but they were only half empty and I did not see that as a big issue.

What I did not realize was that my colleague who worked a full-time shift was putting in overtime because I was late so often, and the morning rush for breakfast was constantly running out of ketchup bottles, and the bowling alley, our primary customer, was getting complaints about slow service to paying customers. I learned about all of this as I was being fired from a job I thought I was great at, and learned my first of many lessons on knowing who your customer is and understanding what the boss really expects and needs.

As in all areas of work, understanding ownership, responsibilities and expected outcomes is critical when implementing any technology. Even more so with Human Resources Technology as it often has dual purposes, multiple end-users, as we covered earlier, and short- and long-term outcome expectations.

The definitions

The Human Resources Technology buyer is generally the role within an organization that owns the primary budget and has the final say on critical HR Technology decisions. Depending on the complexity of the organization and the size of the purchase, this role could be a leadership role in finance, operations, Human Resources or information technology. In exceptionally large organizations this role may also be a shared services leader, HR business unit leaders, HRIT leader, or functional leaders in compensation, learning or talent.

In many organizations buying decisions are handled by HR or IT governance committees made up of representatives from all of these functions, with oversight on policies, practices, risk management, technology and centralized budgets. HR Technology budgets can often be found split across HR, operations and IT – and managed separately from budgets allocated to HR system services or implementation.

A Human Resource information management (HRIM/HRIT) professional is a role that sits at the intersection of HR and technology. This role manages the organization's HR systems strategy, including alignment with HR practices, functions, goals and outcomes. The role is generally responsible for overseeing HR systems selection processes, implementations, maintenance, adoption and innovations.

In 2010, the International Association for Human Resource Information Management (IHRIM) and a third-party validation entity formally confirmed the occupation of HRIM as a profession in which specialized experience and knowledge could be assessed and certified.[1]

The development of a valid certification exam is an immense team effort, one that begins with clear definitions of the knowledge, skills and abilities needed to be competent in a specific professional role. The process includes gathering input from interviews, surveys, obser-vations, group workshops and individual subject matter experts to create a testing blueprint and specific exam questions, all of which must be overseen by professionals trained in psychometric analysis. On a regular cycle, these exams must be evaluated for performance at the overall exam level and individual question level.

The Human Resource Information Professional certification was developed to help organizations select and hire professionals with the requisite knowledge and skillsets required to effectively manage an enterprise HR systems environment. The position has many different titles, including Human Resource information technologist, Human Resource information services and Human Resources information management, but in general these roles are all managing the HR system environments and strategies.

Although a Human Resource information manager role is critical for complex system environments, other roles are important in support-ing HR Technology as well:

- Functional HR support roles are exactly as they sound, they are HR professionals from various HR practice areas that help manage functional-specific setup and maintenance requirements such as business process workflows, change management, adoption and functional reporting. These are sometimes called super-users and are often informal roles.

- HR Technology administration roles are focused on the administrative requirements for implementation and maintenance of HR applicat-ions. They often support system helpdesk environments and help resolve non-technical HR Technology issues that might be caused by configuration settings or data management issues.

- HR Technology infrastructure roles are resources that may sit in IT or HR and are responsible for the more technical aspects of HR Technology implementation and maintenance. This role may have programming duties and be responsible for integrations, technical updates and system testing and security.

The history of HR Technology ownership

The birth of enterprise applications started with organizations implementing large mainframe environments to automate cumbersome paper-based processes across every business function possible, including Human Resources. Early on, these new HR applications were identified as being different from other IT applications focused on small internal populations. In larger organizations, management of these HR applications required a hybrid information management and Human Resources role with a unique mixture of functional HR knowledge and IT specialization. This new Human Resources information management professional oversaw massive company-wide implementations, which included unique regional or business unit customizations and reporting requirements that could stagger the imagination. Over time, as HR applications branched into critical employee- and manager-facing tools, these professionals also became experts at managing myriad variations in security roles, a disarray of integration points, along with multiple levels of user experience requirements. This was not a job for the faint of heart.

These new specialized roles had neither formal education offering nor standard job description from one company to the next, and most experts were self-taught professionals. It was in this environment that IHRIM came into existence: a group of like-minded individuals who got together and developed an association that would focus on the networking and education for this emerging role. In this environment, IT or information management tended to hold the reins in mandating technology decisions based on enterprise environments, and costly investments required for on-premise systems. HR's technical needs were often the last area of investment in many organizations.

In the early 2000s in the era of cloud-based HR Technology, some organizations tried to reduce their HRIT professional positions, believing that these new environments could be implemented with a few well-trained functional HR roles and vendor resources. In reality, research has now shown that for cloud-based HR Technology environments, HRIT professionals are not only necessary to manage complex implementations and continuous updates of this new deployment model, but their role has grown even more strategic, overseeing a complete ecosystem of multiple HR environments, vendors, data privacy standards and security requirements.

The Sapient Insights 2020–2021 HR Systems Survey, 23rd Annual Edition showed that HRIT professionals in all cloud HR Technology environments were 1.5 times more likely to be responsible for data security and configuration decisions over IT or functional roles in older mainframe or on-premise HR Technology environments (see Figure 4.1). The world has shifted, and functional ownership and support are now the most critical elements of maintaining applications, but it creates challenges for data standards, integration standards and enterprise. As functional responsibilities increase, so does budgetary ownership – and more HR Technology budgets are being housed in the HR function or a shared services function than in IT as well.

FIGURE 4.1 Who is responsible for HR system data security and configuration decisions?

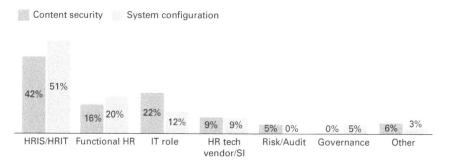

SOURCE Sapient Insights 2020–2021 HR Systems Survey, 23rd Annual Edition

Why you need to care

HR applications impact all aspects of an organization's operations, are likely to be used by nearly every employee, and possibly extend to vendors and contractors. Taking the time to define the outcomes you expect from your HR systems implementation, in terms of your enterprise strategy, always pays off. To achieve this, you need to have clear ownership of the implementation process and governance over the major functionality decisions. Organizations that have clear leadership in their HR Technology efforts and consider the long-term impact of systems on their mission, goals and workforce are more likely to select applications that grow with them and respond to what makes their organization unique.

Organizations often focus solely on specific functionality desired from HR Technology and supporting processes but may overlook how that functionality will actually work within their unique culture. Technology is of little value if not used – it must fit within the context of how an organization operates and how decisions are made to optimize the investment. The footprint of workforce data goes beyond business applications – it extends into social networks, mingles with environmental tools and overlaps with personal profiles. As seen in Figure 4.2, data governance is a major factor in the design of your HR Technology environment as it defines how you capture, access, use, protect and eventually purge necessary data. HR Technology should help you achieve the most value from your workforce data while ensuring adherence to ethical and legal standards.

For example, a large global technical company had an online job board and application process that every candidate was required to complete. The application questions could be tailored based on the job and the candidate's location, but it required setup and configuration to maintain. A US-based candidate was applying for a US-based position and was horrified to find that the application was asking about religious affiliation, so they posted the application form on social media. The outcry and reactions were swift. The organization quickly investigated and found that the cause was a configuration

FIGURE 4.2   Foundational element of HR Technology ownership

Three foundational elements are at the centre of a blueprint:

1. Strategy

2. Culture

3. Data governance

setting that had been turned on for a country that did allow the question and used the data to address discrimination issues in that particular country. Still it was not legal to ask this question in the US, causing the company to face not only face possible fines and legal issues but also the social impact to their brand.

Configuration and security settings play a major role in the adoption, usefulness and regulatory risk that an organization is taking with applications that have direct connections to their workforce and extended audiences.

The other important factor in the issue of ownership is about clearly defining who is responsible for achieving outcomes from this investment. An HR systems environment that is focused on administrative tasks for the HR function and mitigating risks is unlikely to be valued and feel important to senior leadership, managers and employees. Remember that comment about knowing who your real customer is? Well, it is always the organization, not HR. If value creation and outcomes are your goal in HR, then your HR systems environment needs to be adopted, used and have a clear role in helping to run the business and provide value to employees. Ownership isn't just about running the system and making the decisions, it is also about being responsible for the outcomes.

HANDS-ON ACTIVITIES

- Identify who owns your HR Technology budget.
- Identify what is and is not included in that HR Technology budget.
- Discuss with senior leaders how HR Technology expenditures are requested and approved.
- Discuss with your HR Technology leaders the major criteria your organization has for investing in technology.
- Question whether your organization has a standard process for deciding to increase HR Technology budgets.

Endnote

1 IHRIM (2021) Exam overview and fees, https://ihrim.org/education/hrip-certification/exam-overview-and-fees/ (archived at https://perma.cc/Q9T3-5ZTG)

05

Core HR administration applications

Introduction

My first major HR Technology project was for a large retail organization, with over 25,000 employees. We were tasked with doing a major upgrade of the on-premise payroll and HRMS environment and getting it completed before the frenzied holiday buying season began. There was added pressure in the project because just five years earlier when the organization first implemented the entire enterprise resource planning solution, which included finance, HR and supply chain applications, the project had gone poorly, causing a lack of product in the stores during the crucial holiday season and literally bringing the organization to a halt in managing both finances and payroll during its busiest season. As we began our upgrade project, which was expected to last more than nine months from start to finish, every meeting started off with whispered stories of what had gone wrong in the first implementation and a clear mandate to make sure this upgrade was managed differently.

One of the first things we learned about what went wrong with the first project was the implementation team's lack of respect for existing administration-level employees. These employees were not included in early process mapping, configuration or testing efforts – and because of that, critical steps were missed and important requirements were overlooked in the original implementation effort. This time around my job was to be the primary liaison between the payroll and benefits function and the IT department, ensuring clear communications and early involvement in all critical decisions and testing efforts. Like most people, up to this point in my career I did not think much about the process of payroll and benefits as long as my correct pay cheque showed up every two weeks. That all changed after spending a full week doing a job analysis of the payroll and benefits team in the large, windowless room they occupied, with the constant hum of computers, printing machines and the server room on the other side of the wall. This team was amazing, and they loved their jobs.

The workload was split up into regions, audit teams, special issues and program management so that there was a constant flow of data entry, data checking and auditing going on throughout the day – and a general acceptance that the data coming in from the field would always have errors and require constant review and cleaning. Within one week, I realized this function probably knew this organization better than anyone else, including the CEO and HR leaders. They had data at their fingertips and knew everything from vulnerable stores to the most engaged departments. They could tell by the number of time-entry errors they got per store location that required pay cheque adjustments which stores would have future high turnover rates, and by how many compensation ranges were being adjusted up or down which divisions were having the hardest time finding skilled workers. They knew which benefits were being used and adopted the most, and they knew which areas of the organization had the highest levels of leave requests. They were also aware of which government regulations caused us the most work inside the organization and which areas constituted our greatest compliance risks. With all this knowledge, they were rarely asked for data beyond payroll accuracy numbers, enrolment numbers and actual spend amounts – and no one seemed to realize that their data was often leading indicators of issues or opportunities versus the lagging indicators they pulled from operation systems.

As we worked on the upgrade project, they were conscientious testers and excellent at process analysis, understanding where the data came from and where it ended up and at what point we saw the greatest errors. Our upgrade went off without any major issues, on time and just slightly over budget – partially because our team pushed for a major celebration at the end of the process that included everyone who worked on the initiative, especially our payroll and benefits team.

The definitions

FIGURE 5.1   Core HR administrative applications category

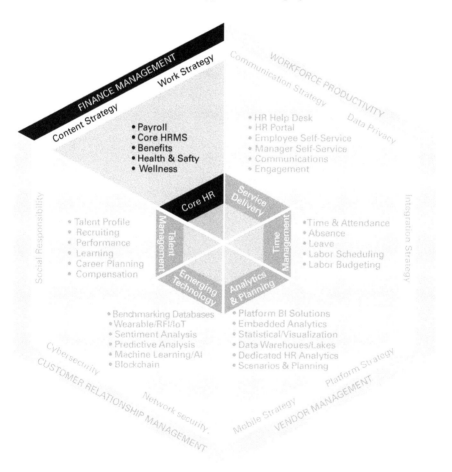

The HR systems journey generally starts by deploying core HR administrative applications as seen in Figure 5.1, initially in the form of a payroll solution – over 93 per cent of organizations have a payroll solution in place[1] or outsource both the services and the payroll application. Payroll solutions are often implemented with an HRMS, but payroll systems can stand alone, leveraging basic data-capturing capabilities in place of an HRMS until an organization needs to expand. Just over 87 per cent of surveyed organizations have an HRMS in use today. For most organizations, the payroll and HRMS applications sit at the heart of their HR and workforce data management needs, sharing data with multiple HR applications. Rounding out this category of critical HR applications for most organizations are the employee health and safety, wellness and benefits applications.

As noted in Figure 5.2, core HR applications are widely adopted across all organization types, with over 80 per cent of organizations currently using all three of these applications.

Payroll administration application

The payroll application manages, organizes and automates your workforce payments, streamlining the entire process from scheduling, record-keeping, calculating taxes and deductions to processing the actual payment. Like all HR systems, the available solutions in the market can range from simple offerings designed for a single industry to highly configurable solutions that can handle multiple

FIGURE 5.2   Core HR application adoption data, 2020

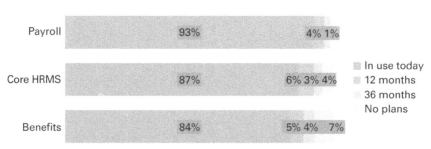

SOURCE Sapient Insights, 2020–2021 HR Systems Survey, 23rd Annual Edition

business models and regional requirements. In the case of payroll applications, it is imperative that an organization thoroughly understands its needs and selects a solution that can meet those needs – making a wrong decision can at best cost you disgruntled employees and at worst place your organization at risk of falling foul of local tax regulations and employment laws.

The main features of a payroll application generally include:

- Payroll setup and record-keeping – an environment that allows an organization to set up company-wide payroll standards, like when and how often payroll will run and what benefits are given to everyone, such as mobile phone stipend. It also obtains data on new employees, their status, their pay rate, their legal documentation, tax withholdings and benefits.

- Payroll processing engine – literally runs the payroll process and computes an employee's net income by subtracting taxes, retirement savings, insurance and other deductions from the original gross income.

- Tax engine – payroll processing cannot happen without a regularly updated tax engine, which maintains tax tables for a payroll application for tax changes such as rates, tax laws and tax limits. Some payroll solutions manage their own tax engine, while others outsource the tax engine to other larger vendors in this space. Tax engines become even more complex when you are managing global payroll issues, and usually each country has a few local organizations that keep track of local tax tables, that multiple vendors work with to access their tax engines.

- Withholding process management – once the employees' net income is calculated and dispersed, the amount subtracted through withholding needs to be dispersed to the appropriate entities, for example taxes to government entities, retirement funds or benefits suppliers. Some organizations outsource this while others manage the effort internally.

- Compliance and regulation management database – a mixture of an application and services in which the payroll solution provider gives content on constantly changing local, state, federal and regional employment laws, and where appropriate automatically updates the software to address those regulations or prompts a review by the organization.

- Tax filing or reporting – tax filing functionality in payroll software will allow you to calculate the local government taxes your business owes, file your return and generate appropriate tax forms for your employees based on their local regulations.

Human Resource management system

This is one term that can be highly confusing in the HR Technology space as vendors often use the term as a single application, a suite of applications or an entire HR Technology category. At its most basic level, the HRMS, also sometimes called a Human Resource Information System (HRIS), is a record-keeping and workflow application. Its primary function is to store all the relevant HR information on your workforce, your organizational reporting structure, your data security standards and your data privacy standards. The application also requires data input tools and workflow solutions that allow the organization to capture, maintain, approve changes and audit the information on a regular basis.

For small organizations some of this data management can be done inside the payroll application, but as organizations grow and become more complex, an HRMS is required to be a central hub for information, a single place for integrations, updates and reporting. The primary location for accessing and reporting workforce information, this application also generally includes the organization's single point of truth concerning security access, organizational structure and individual employee profile data. In larger organizations, they might use both the HRMS data as well as the company's Active Directory data to authenticate who should have access to specific software applications, dashboards, or reports.

Benefits administration application

Benefits administration applications are one of the most diverse HR application categories around the globe and generally allow an organization to create, maintain and manage the use of its non-payroll benefits programmes. Non-payroll employee benefits structures vary greatly around the world. For example, employees can be offered pension or retirement options, health insurance and/or other health and welfare benefits (such as reimbursement accounts or employee assistance programmes), and voluntary/flexible benefits (which can range from supplemental health coverage to childcare vouchers or car schemes). There are underlying applications for all these benefits, but the majority of these solutions focus on one benefits area for one country or region.

Outsourcing models

Outsourcing is the process of paying a third-party organization to obtain goods or services that were traditionally done in-house. Generally, this is done to reduce costs and improve efficiencies. HR functions have a long history of outsourcing the more administrative aspects of their work, particularly administration of payroll, HR record-keeping and benefits administration.

Still, there is no hard-and-fast rule around outsourcing, and organizations have choices over how their payroll, HR record-keeping and benefits activities are managed. The services can be performed completely in-house, partially outsourced to a third party (ie co-sourced) or fully outsourced to a third party. Many small organizations start off outsourcing almost everything, by leverage co-employment models like a PEO within the United States or a GEO outside the United States.

Outsourced payroll services often include activities such as payroll data entry and validation, payroll processing, and tax filing and reporting. Outsourced benefits services include activities such as managing benefits enrolment, regulatory reporting, education and strategic planning. Organizations also have to decide whether they bundle benefits with payroll services or combine those functions with consulting or brokerage services in a comprehensive outsourcing arrangement. On average, today about 30 per cent of the market is co-sourcing payroll or benefits administration, while just over 12 per cent are fully outsourcing these functions, outside of PEO/GEO arrangements.[2]

An organization's decision to outsource is often dependent on where and when the actual funds from payroll and benefits disbursements are handled. Many outsourcing vendors make their largest profits not from billing for the outsourcing services but from the payroll float time. The float is the difference between the time the vendor receives the payroll funds and the time they actually have to disperse the fund through a payroll check. That timeframe can mean a large amount of money being accrued in interest before an employee actually cashes their check. The emerging trend towards instant and on-demand pay options is having an impact on some of the float financial metrics but is being offset by increased use and transaction fees that are often charged for the convenience of early access to an employee's pay cheque.

The history of core HR administrative applications

Core HR administration processes of payroll management, Human Resource data management and benefits management were among the first HR practices to be automated and moved into a digital format, as we discussed in the earlier section on historical timelines.

Originally these applications were designed to reduce paperwork, time and manual effort required to pay employees and record sensitive personal identification information. These applications were designed solely for the HR administrative staff; employees and managers were never expected to use these systems. Although these applications improved timelines, there was no such thing as real-time process management – everything still had to be manually sent to the HR or payroll administration staff to enter into the system. To address this issue the term 'effective dating' became critical in HR.

EXAMPLE

An employee might get a pay rise on 1 October but the paperwork does not make it to HR until 15 October. The paychecks for that month have already run. HR enters the pay rise, effectively dates it for the 1st and checks that the system adds an increase for October and November to the pay cheque run for November.

Effective dating is the date upon which something is considered to take effect. It may be a past, present or future date, and it can be different from the date when the event occurs or is recorded.

Effective dating allowed these new HR applications to manage a multi-dimensional view of time for every bit of data and enabled systems to create an audit trail for timeline changes.

Over time, organizations realized that they could become even more efficient by granting employees and management direct access to these applications so that they could enter their own information and access data as needed. Since the HR administrative areas and the employee/management areas of these applications evolved along separate timelines, depending on the age or maturity of the administrative applications, these two areas (HR administration and employee/manager self-service) may be separate applications with different design elements and maintenance schedules. These applications may also have different effective dating or record auditing standards.

The complexity of these administrative efforts has grown even more challenging as the ease of travel and technology have allowed even the smallest organizations to begin to work globally, outside of their headquarters location. The greater the mix of professions and locations, the greater the range of compensation models and regulatory requirements, the more difficult it is to administer.

The US Department of Labor administers and enforces more than 180 federal laws that can impact workplace activities, and that number only expands when you add state and local regulations. European labour laws provide many benefits and employee protections that require careful payroll and benefits administration that are not offered in other countries. While countries require specific employee demographic data such as age, race or sexual orientation be captured and shared with government databases, other countries specifically prohibit capturing certain demographic data.

No payroll provider can claim to be completely capable of handling all global payroll situations – with roughly 200 sovereign nations, there are conflicting laws covering who gets paid what, when and in which currency. Most multinational organizations have multiple payroll solutions to address different requirements in each country, often leading organizations to have no environment that allows them to see all their payroll data rolled up into a single environment. The payroll vendor ADP comes the closest to a full global solution provider – a provider with a wide network of partners, regional data centres, flexible applications and payroll aggregator solutions. Similarly, traditionally there have been no benefits applications that can manage every country's standard benefits programmes, leaving organizations to rely on multiple suppliers here as well.

Many organizations have multiple HRMS, payroll and benefits applications – sometimes because of the many global requirements that force them to use different solutions and in other cases because of an organization's long history of mergers and acquisitions. In either case, running multiple HRMS, payroll and benefits applications creates duplicate work, highly siloed work environments, difficulties in conducting enterprise workforce planning, and challenges with providing internal mobility opportunities for existing employees.

In all these application areas, we are starting to see solutions that provide integration and aggregation capabilities, which means organizations continue to use their local service providers or multiple environments but through system integrations the data (not the actual processing) is rolled up into a single payroll or HRMS environment, allowing for a holistic view of these critical data sets.

Why you need to care

Core HR administration processes like payroll, HR record-keeping and benefits are some of the most important business processes your company performs, yet some of the least understood by anyone outside of HR.

These applications impact an organization's most valuable resource on a fundamental level. In almost any other area, 99 per cent accuracy would be amazing – but in payroll, HR record-keeping or benefits, a 99.5 per cent effectiveness rate means major issues for employees:

- Five employees with an incorrect pay cheque might not be able to pay rent, put food on the table or fuel in their car that week.
- An employee with a sick child may not be able to access an after-hours nurse offered in their benefits package, due to a miscoded benefit option.
- A national health crisis hits while multiple employees are travelling overseas and several become ill, but an outdated emergency contact form leaves the company unable to get in touch with the employee's family.

A priority for any business is that administration of payroll, HR record-keeping and benefits is executed flawlessly. Many organizations that manage their own payroll process in-house make trial runs a week in advance of the actual payroll run, to assess for any errors or audit issues they can catch prior to the actual event.

As noted earlier, administration of payroll and benefits produces more data than most organizations realize, and it is the most accurate and thorough picture of the workforce and the work they accomplish for the organization. The absolute necessity for perfection also ensures that the data is clean and accurate in a way that is often not the case in other HR applications. A well-run payroll and benefits administration function can provide some of the most accurate and forward-looking data sets for assessing:

- employment status;
- verified work hours;
- increasing turnover;
- increasing overtime;
- reductions in productivity;
- low engagement levels.

More traditional workforce analytics efforts require assumption and research to produce usable data for critical decisions, whereas payroll and benefits administration data provides immediate access to information that is often overlooked.

On average, organizations will keep a core HR administrative application for anywhere from 6 to 10 years, and that number continues to increase for large global organizations.[3] Getting to know these applications and the teams that manage these processes daily will provide a much-needed reality check on the scale and scope of the HR organization's actual impact and work within an organization. Newer, more user-friendly versions of these applications, with 24/7 cloud access, are entering the market rapidly, providing more accurate and current data, improved workflows, better end-user experiences and easier integration with other enterprise applications. It is now possible to understand the exact monetary value of the payroll obligation an organization has at any given moment, and for employees to have constant access to the important information they need concerning their pay cheque, benefits and personal information accessible to their employer.

HANDS-ON ACTIVITIES

- Get a total number of employees who are expected to receive a pay cheque in your organization's next pay cycle.

- Identify the applications in use currently and whether they are part of a suite of technologies, point solution or completely outsourced (if your organization uses more than these applications, create additional rows).

TABLE 5.1

HR administrative applications	Application use and deployment model				
	Not in use	ERP suite	HR suite	Point solution	Totally outsourced
Payroll application					
HRMS application					
Benefits application					

- IF they are in use, list the name and implementation data of all your current payroll, HRMS and benefits applications:

  ○ Payroll _____

  ○ HRMS _____

  ○ Benefits _____

- If you are using an HRMS application, get a total number of active employee profiles in the application.

- If you are using a benefits application, get a total number of benefits packages managed in the application.

- Identify any workforce groups that are not included in the HRMS application currently and why (for example, contingent workforces or third-party temporary workers may not be included).

- If any of the applications are part of an outsourcing agreement, list the name of major outsource vendors and services offered.

- Assess the current level of satisfaction your payroll, benefits and HR administrators have with how the current applications handle the processes below on a scale of 1 (terrible) to 5 (excellent) – this can be assessed through discussion, interviews, surveys or your personal observations.

Payroll administrators:

- entering new employees into the payroll system

- processing payroll

- auditing payroll

Benefits administrators:

- adding new benefits packages/offerings

- managing open enrolment for benefits packages

- auditing benefits selections

HR administrators

- entering a new employee into the HRMS system

- setting up a workflow for gathering information from employees

- validating new employee-entered data

CASE STUDY
The human side of HR systems

In 2005, the hurricane season was one of significant disturbance and destruction. Lockheed Martin has several business units in the southeastern United States as well as 2,800 employees, and these were in the direct path of many hurricanes that year. When Hurricane Katrina tore through New Orleans and surrounding areas, Lockheed Martin business units and their employees were devastated. The HR Services team and volunteers were overwhelmed with trying to operate the phone lines to take care of their employees and business units.

The team reached out to their outsource provider, Affiliated Computer Services, Inc (ACS). It partnered with them to set up a system that could handle the daily phone calls and emails the team received from employees. This new system could take the overwhelming amount of phone calls and capture employee information. The Lockheed Martin team focused on other hurricane-related issues such as housing, donations and benefits delivery by creating this system. The volunteers were only able to handle 1,000 phone calls across three locations, whereas the system was able to take in 7,000 phone calls over several weeks. The information logged in the central database was accessible to the ACS and Lockheed Martin teams with up-to-the-minute updates.

On 20 September 2005, less than a month after the storm hit, all 2,800 employees could be accounted for. The team then set their sights on creating a method for affected employees to secure necessary funds and housing. They designed and deployed an easy online system for employees to contribute to the Lockheed Martin Employee Assistance Fund via payroll deduction. More than $4.2 million had been paid out to affected employees for essential needs by the end of the year. The hard work and long hours involved in the combined effort by the Lockheed Martin/ACS hurricane relief team made a significant difference in people's lives.[4]

CASE STUDY
The human side of payroll

Hurricane Sandy hit lower Manhattan late in the evening on 29 October 2012. The flooding from the heavy rain and high winds destroyed a power substation that drove the city into darkness. Due to the power outage, any type of voice or data communication was spotty at best. One of the businesses affected by the storm was a non-profit home healthcare company. The employees included nurses, therapists and social workers who would spend their time visiting patients and providing treatments throughout the five boroughs of New York City.

As the storm approached, the city shut down and declared a state of emergency. The healthcare company's employees made sure patients were taken care of to the best of their ability and the company urged everyone to stay home while the storm hit. However, once the storm was over, these nurses, therapists and social workers would have to get back into the communities to check on their patients. The problem was that many of these employees lived pay cheque to pay cheque and would need money to get out to do their jobs. The company knew it would have to try to run payroll (payday was only a couple of days away before the storm hit) despite Hurricane Sandy's aftermath. The payroll administrators knew what they had to do, but how do you run payroll when you do not have access to the internet due to a significant city-wide power outage?

Luckily, the company had moved its workforce and payroll systems into the cloud in prior years, which meant there was little to no downtime before getting things rolling. The payroll manager called the payroll support desk, hoping to get an answer on what to do. After hundreds of attempts to get through, the manager finally was able to speak to the support desk manager. The support desk manager was then able to connect the payroll manager to a Toronto consultant who had worked with the team previously and knew their system. The consultant could get into their payroll system and get everything arranged to pay the employees on time.

As we noted earlier, there is no room for errors or excuses when it comes to an employee's paycheck, and that includes natural disasters. Organizations that understand the critical nature of their payroll applications have clear disaster recovery plans as well as procedures ensuring employees or contract workers are cross-trained and ready to jump in at critical times to ensure the employees' greatest needs are met and a business can maintain operations in the most challenging situations.[5]

Endnotes

1 Sapient Insights 2020–2021 HR Systems Survey White Paper, 23rd Annual Edition

2 Sapient Insights Group, 2020–2021 HR Systems Survey, Voice of Customer Payroll and Benefits White Paper

3 Sapient Insights, 2020–2021 HR Systems Survey, 23rd Annual Edition

4 Dierkes, J (nd) Anticipating the Unexpected, *SSO Network*, www.ssonetwork. com/business-process-outsourcing/articles/anticipating-the-unexpected (archived at https://perma.cc/8B5M-KXUW)

5 Clements, B (2019) Can You Run Payroll in the Eye of a Hurricane? *Workforce Institute*, https://workforceinstitute.org/can-you-run-payroll-in-the-eye-of-a-hurricane/ (archived at https://perma.cc/HL5B-YGZH)

06

HR service delivery applications

Introduction

The average employee will work between 60,000 and 100,000 hours in a lifetime, depending on industry, region and personal circumstances; only sleep takes more time in our lives. The enormity of this fact is even more significant when you consider the wall that has been placed between our personal and professional lives – even if you work in a country with mandated flexibility and support for families, organizations still expect delineation between our work and personal activities.

Early in my career, I was introduced to the idea that work and personal life should be separate – it was simply how things were done. HR provided basic services to everyone and offered out-of-the-box standard benefits required either by regulation or industry expectations. With yesterday's technology, this was the extent to which an organization could accommodate my personal life when managing thousands of employees, each with their own unique needs. Although delineation was expected between work and personal life, as the agreed-upon social contract, that line quickly became blurred with the onset of new technology that enabled 24/7 connections to both our work and social environments and led to our personal and work worlds being more closely connected than ever before.

In 2014, the constant line that I had drawn between my personal and professional life was shattered when my husband was diagnosed with an inoperable form of cancer that would take his life just two short years later. In a single moment, I went from being an average employee for whom the standard benefits and basic HR services met most of my needs to an uncommon employee facing the most difficult time of my life, and in desperate need of information and services only available from HR. My employer at the time was a small consulting firm with a highly distributed workforce and a small HR function that was often overstretched but tried hard to deliver adequate HR.

Like most families today, mine had already accepted that my work was part of our lives, sometimes out of balance, but not often – the 24/7 makeup of my work meant that I could be more flexible in where I worked and when I spent time with my family. In return for making myself constantly available to work via phone and virtual conferencing environments, and my family's flexibility, I think I had an unrealistic expectation that work would similarly be available in my greatest hour of need.

All of a sudden, I needed constant access to my healthcare benefits information, immediate access to an employee assistance program that could help me find mental healthcare for everyone in my family, and a flexible schedule that allowed me to continue to work while attending doctors' visits and chemotherapy sessions. In the midst of this, I needed to communicate my situation to HR, and needed help communicating my needs to work colleagues and leadership. When we realized the treatments were not working, I needed immediate access to family leave options, a clear understanding of how that would impact our family financials, and help rearranging workloads. Eventually, I needed a work environment that provided support and stability while grief engulfed my life, and my teammates needed guidance on how to balance my needs with their workloads and business expectations.

Instead of easy 24/7 access to these HR services, I ended up spending hours on the phone trying to get through to the one person who could approve something or give me the information I needed. Instead of well-organized online information or outreaches from HR when I needed the most help, I found pages of PDF policy documentation and silence. Don't get me wrong, the company itself was full of kind and understanding people, who tried desperately to help and give me as much flexibility as possible. The issue was simply that many of our HR services were built to be reactionary in nature and the information was locked away in on-premise environments accessible only by an already stretched HR staff. We had rolled out the bare minimum in employee self-service tools and required our benefit providers to have even fewer support methods.

Although healthcare issues are generally a bigger issue in the United States, HR is the central point of information for all kinds of benefits and services that we often take for granted until our lives are turned upside down. No matter the services or solutions offered by your HR organization – wellness tools, financial planning, learning, mentoring, payroll deposits, time-off options, internal job postings – if they are not accessible when and where employees need them, they go unused. When organizations invest in HR services that are rarely used, it is a double loss in money spent, lost productivity and lost trust between the employee and the employer.

The definitions

HR service delivery applications are an ever-evolving HR systems category, as seen in Figure 6.1, that focuses on helping an HR function deliver the wide range of services it provides to various stakeholders throughout an organization. These applications manage the HR experience, communication, content and data sharing that are part of an HR organization's service delivery model.

There is a multitude of ways in which an HR function can deliver its services to employees, managers, executives and extended audiences. Service delivery models are selected based on various organizational factors, including size, industry, geographical distribution, capabilities of employees/managers, available technology and culture. A single standard service delivery model may be put in place for everyone, or organizations may use hybrid models that mix multiple models across different stakeholder groups. Common types of HR service delivery models in use today include those shown in Table 6.1

When core HR applications are adopted, there is naturally some level of HR administrative efficiency achieved and these applications usually come with some basic support or additional modules for employee-facing service delivery. However, as organizations increase in size and complexity, they often need to expand beyond their core

FIGURE 6.1   HR service delivery applications category

HR applications to stand-alone HR service delivery tools or a suite of HR service delivery applications.

There is still much debate in the industry as to the exact applications that fall into this emerging HR systems category and whether they are stand-alone applications or should be combined into a single platform, but the most common applications include the following:

HR portal applications – a single online location accessible only to employees, a gateway to access HR-related information, systems,

TABLE 6.1   Service delivery models

Service delivery models	Definitions
Shared service centres	Centralized point of HR services (and possible non-HR services) into a single function focused on reducing redundant work, generally providing services through a call centre environment. May report outside of HR.
Centres of excellence	A team of specialized professionals (recruiting, strategic planning, learning) organized as a central unit that does not sit in any one function but works across the organization as a whole. Generally provides services on a project basis. May report into HR or a shared services function.
HR generalists	When an HR professional has a broad range of HR responsibilities and provides HR services across the organization as needed. Generally reports into the HR function.
HR business partners	When an HR professional is embedded into an organization's functions for the purposes of helping to link the functions' strategy with the HR strategy and services. Usually reports jointly to the HR and the function they support.
Self-service applications	Technology interfaces and workflows designed to allow HR clients to obtain services without interacting with an HR representative. Generally supported by HRIT or shared service function.
Digital assistants/chatbots	Technology designed with some form of workflow, advanced computer programming and machine learning capabilities to anticipate and offer services needed based on personal inputs. Generally supported by HRIT, IT or shared service function.

content and communication. Newer versions of these applications are tailored to an individual role or personal profile, providing a more tailored HR experience. These are sometimes purchased and maintained as stand-alone solutions, and in other cases they are modules within an existing HR or ERP environment.

Employee self-service (ESS) – an administrative application that allows an employee to directly manage their personal information and complete HR tasks, guides employees through HR process work-flows and accesses relevant HR data for the employee. In some cases, these have similar features to an HR portal, but the primary role of these applications is data entry and validation, and process work-flows. If this is not automatically delivered with an HRMS, it may be a separate module within an HR suite, or it may be part of an HR service delivery platform that feeds the information directly to an HRMS or payroll application.

Manager self-service (MSS) – an administrative application that allows a manager to facilitate management activities for their direct-report employees, initiate employment-related actions, collect critical management data, approve employee requests and access workforce reporting. Deploying a module like this assumes that managers have the capacity and capabilities to manage tasks that traditionally may have been managed by the HR function. Similar to the ESS applica-tion, if this is not automatically delivered with an HRMS, it may be a separate module within an HR suite or be part of an HR service platform.

HR content management applications – software that streamlines the process for content creation and management. It helps organiza-tions create, receive, track, manage and store HR documentation for legal and policy purposes. These applications generally include work-flow and electronic signature capabilities, and tools for auditing and reporting on the document management process. In some cases, these are purchased as stand-alone solutions or as part of HR portals, help-desk solutions or communication solutions.

Employee helpdesk/case management applications – software that supports the facilitation, tracking and resolution of HR inquiries and requests for help made by employees, usually to a shared service centre function. These are sometimes known as ticketing solutions and often have workflow tools that allow for tiered levels of support and responses based on the difficulty of the case being addressed. These are generally bought as stand-alone solutions and are often standard IT helpdesk software with adjustments made for HR privacy requirements and workflows.

HR communication and feedback applications – software that facilitates two-way communication with employees, including feedback and engagement surveys, creating communication content and managing employee communication workflow. Sometimes these include tools for collaboration, social communication and even employee rewards depending on the focus of the application.

These are critical data-collection and information-sharing tools that are tightly connected to a workforce's ability to achieve talent, HR and even business outcomes. As seen in Figure 6.2, organizations are most likely to adopt existing employee self-service applications, but areas like communication and feedback tools are still adopted by just slightly over 50 per cent of the market. Either way, the 85 per cent of organizations that invest in at least one service delivery application see higher levels of employee engagement and system adoption, along with increased HR efficiencies.[1]

These applications are significantly influenced by consumer trends and employee expectations for emerging technologies.

FIGURE 6.2   HR service delivery application adoption data, 2020

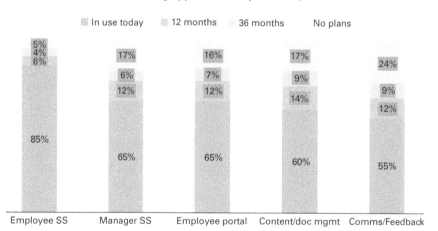

The history of HR service delivery applications

This HR Technology category started almost 20 years ago as a simple self-service add-on module to either the payroll or HRMS application, and that original concept of creating self-service access for employees, managers and extended audiences like candidates expanded into every HR Technology that has come to market since then.

Deploying these early self-service modules was viewed as a way to improve the efficiency of an HR function while keeping the organization compliant with local regulations on reporting labour data. Early on it was clear that organizations that implemented any form of employee and manager self-service applications were able to increase the size of the employee population served without increasing HR headcount. Efficiency is always a positive outcome, but if that was the primary goal for HR organizations, then we quickly would have seen 100 per cent adoption of these applications soon after their release. In point of fact, it took almost 10 years for employee self-service applications to achieve 85 per cent adoption, and today only 65 per cent of organizations have rolled out manager self-service applications. What was the roadblock to adoption?

Before the self-service applications were rolled out, this administrative HR work and data-collection activities were kicked off by filling out a paper-based form and then passed off to the HR staff to manage and complete. As self-service applications became the norm, both employees and managers started to take note of the additional time they were investing in completing tasks and constantly maintaining data inside these new HR systems, creating efficiency issues in other areas of the company. HR staff also started to take note of the growing errors or incorrect information being entered by employees and managers alike and grew concerned over the level of data cleaning and auditing required to ensure local compliance and correct data reporting.

Efficiency and compliance requirements were important issues, but so was the client experience, return on effort and the actual outcome of the work. Millions of dollars were being invested in these enterprise applications, with growing expectations that they would help more effectively run an organization. To achieve this outcome, these systems needed to be filled with data and used on a regular basis. To make these systems important to end-users, organizations started to leverage self-service technology to improve workflow processes and speed up decision making. They incentivized its accurate use through regular reporting and focused on improving the overall user's experience. The focus for self-service tools quickly shifted from efficiency metrics for HR To a focus on enterprise process improvements, usefulness of captured data, speed of decision making and reporting capabilities.

As the industry shifted the focus of HR Technology from capturing legal and administrative data to providing communications and expanded HR services, buyers began to focus even more attention on the end-user experiences. With every screen and output of today's modern HR system, a service interaction is taking place. For each employee, the service interaction encompasses the ease of access, interface look and feel, and total process workflow – and consumer technology sets these expectations. Meanwhile, an employee's individual needs and motivators set the expectations for desired outcomes and return on effort. These changes have led to the expansion of the category beyond simple self-service tools into what is universally known as HR service delivery and recently coined terms like 'employee experience platforms'.

Emerging technology has an impact on all areas of HR Technology but is most easily observed in action in the HR service delivery category. Critical emerging technology tools such as mobile, social, artificial intelligence and augmented reality are already deeply embedded in this category of HR Technology. Mobile access makes it easier and more convenient for managers and employees to retrieve their information and get help when they need it. Access to social communication channels provides a deeper sense of community and rewards information sharing. Wearables and work embedded tracking technology provides an easy way to capture data on work environment and activities and give useful feedback for both employees and organizations. Digital assistants offer a less labour-intensive approach to updating and maintaining data, and when you add machine learning this creates a personal experience with guidance on next steps tailored to the employee's needs.

Emerging technologies are a critical part of making the HR service delivery application category more valuable to organizations and end-users alike. It also opens a plethora of critical issues organizations must address concerning biased data sets, data privacy standards, governance over the ethical use of passively captured information, and personal data security. It is important to realize that workforce regulations around the globe rarely keep up with the speed of emerging technology, and organizations that rely solely on meeting the minimum requirements in addressing these concerns based on local regulations will likely find themselves on the wrong side of history and open themselves up to future legal actions. Instead, address these issues like any other organization innovation. Conduct a solid risk assessment and put in place standards that match your culture and brand, and imagine it was your family member using these tools – what level of trust and security would you expect from the company?

Why you need to care

In order to stay competitive and attract a workforce that is passionate and motivated, organizations need to redirect the HR conversation from compliance and risk to one of experience and outcomes. Today's workforce demands more personal attention; they understand the value of their own knowledge and skills, and they thrive on opportunities to use their capabilities and increase their experiences. Employees are looking for a work environment that allows them to blend their personal goals with their professional careers, and organizations that tap into these new expectations and change their relationship with their workforce will find an amazing new level of interest from their engaged employees. Understanding this new workforce, and how to harness its enthusiasm, becomes a critical requirement for organizations that hope to increase productivity, sustain long-term growth and innovate during the most challenging times.

When leveraged well, HR service delivery applications provide us with a scalable way to build this new workforce relationship, based on trust, transparency and mutual respect for the outcomes both entities hope to achieve. When leveraged poorly, this primary connection point to employees can also be frustrating, hard to use, feel invasive and quickly lower employee engagement.

A study completed in 2018 with workforces in 46 countries from several large organizations found that many employees are unaware of all the self-service options they have available, or how they can leverage HR service delivery applications effectively. Every one of these organizations had widely deployed employee self-service, manager self-service, HR helpdesk solutions and content management solutions in place at the time of this survey.

- 92 per cent of employees actually completed at least one employee self-service task online.

- 32 per cent of Asia-based employees and 35 per cent of European-based employees did not know that they had the ability to swap shifts or change withholdings online, compared with 18 per cent of US-based employees.

- Employees were most likely to contact their manager to request vacation and sick leave time versus using an employee self-service tool.

- The task most frequently executed by employees on a mobile device was to manage work-related connections, outside of self-service tools.

- Asia-Pacific-based millennial supervisors were the most likely to call HR versus using manager self-service HR Tools.[2]

Each HR process has touch points that when looked at through the lens of personalizing the HR experience can lead to meeting employees where they are – not just on their mobile device but living their lives in real time and conducting business in the real world. In the middle of these debates concerning the role and impact of technology on an organization's ability to optimize its workforce, gather individual data and address a workforce's unique and changing needs, HR service delivery technologies must be given a major portion of this discussion.

As an HR or HRIT practitioner, addressing the topic of creating a consumer-like HR service delivery experience through technology, it is easy to reduce the issue to one of mobility and improved user interfaces. Making HR more accessible is a step in the right direction, but it falls short of what we *should* be doing. HR is much more than just payroll and timesheets, and as the most recent global health crisis has shown, we can reimagine the world without the strict barriers between work and personal environments that we put in place decades ago due to fears of reduced productivity and increased resource requirements from HR. Leveraging today's new technology, we have the opportunity to begin interacting with each employee as an individual, one with a unique set of personal needs inside and outside of work hours. We can reduce the fear through transparency and openness, engaging employees where and when they need HR services the most.

HANDS-ON ACTIVITIES

- Identify the HR service delivery models in use in your organization and whether they are available to the entire organization or to specific functions or regions.

TABLE 6.2

Service delivery models in use	For the entire organization	For specific functions	For specific regions
Shared service centres			
Centres of excellence			
HR generalists			
HR business partners			
Self-service applications			
Digital assistants/chatbots			

- Identify which of these applications are in use currently and whether they are part of a suite of technologies, are a point solution or are completely outsourced (if your organization uses more than these applications, create additional rows).

TABLE 6.3

	Application use and deployment model			
HR service delivery applications	Not in use	ERP suite	HR suite	Point solution
HR employee portal				
Employee self-service (ESS)				
Manager self-service (MSS)				
HR content management				
Employee helpdesk/case management				
HR communication and feedback				

- Think about your latest interaction with any systems that falls under the HR Technology umbrella.
  - Were you happy with your experience with the application?
  - Were you happy with the return on your effort with the application?
  - Did you achieve the outcome you expected or wanted from your interaction with the application?
  - Was that interaction compelling enough to cause a behaviour change?

If you answered no to any of these questions, describe why.

- Randomly choose at least 10 employees/managers in your organization and ask them about their latest interaction with any systems that fall under the HR Technology umbrella.
  - Were you happy with your experience with the application?
  - Were you happy with the return on your effort with the application?
  - Did you achieve the outcome you expected or wanted from your interaction with the application?
  - Was that interaction compelling enough to cause a behaviour change?

If they answered no to any of these questions, ask them to describe why.

- Assess the current perception of your organization's HR service delivery experience for each organizational role listed below on a scale of 1 (terrible) to 5 (excellent) – this can be assessed through discussion, interviews, surveys or your personal observations.

  o HR administration

  o HR business partner/management

  o Senior business executives

  o Managers/supervisors

  o Salaried employees

  o Hourly employees

CASE STUDY
The human side of HR service delivery

A technology company with over 140,000 employees spanning 180 countries was focused on an organizational mission to help transform people's lives through technology. Like most large global organizations, rapid growth and acquisitions had created a complex HR systems architecture which led to challenging HR silos. With over 400 integrations and a divided global workforce, operating on multiple separate instances of cloud and on-demand HR applications, the organization felt it was time to create an HR experience that would support a culture of one company.

The Human Resources team prioritized six requirements they felt would address organizational needs and simplify their HR systems management: highly engaging user experience; sophisticated integration capabilities; simplified infrastructure, so IT and HR could run operations collaboratively; depth and breadth of product capability, for unique current needs; and depth and breadth of roadmap for future product capabilities.

After careful evaluation, the organization chose a leading cloud ERP/HRMS suite for their new core HR solution along with a new HR Service Delivery suite for knowledge, case management and the engagement layer. This meant retiring 40-plus legacy HR tools to support a single, unified and harmonized experience across the board. Although the HRMS company retired a bulk of their existing HR applications, they were keeping a few separate applications not included in their core HR suite such as Time and Attendance. The HR Service Delivery solution would provide the employee portal bringing the experience of the remaining few applications and weave together the employee service experience.

In a little over a year, the company launched the new HR experience with over 250 harmonized processes. The new Employee Service Centre became a single destination that was designed and personalized with knowledge to support each employee's unique HR related needs. The portal and knowledge experience focused on making it easy for employees, to get the answers they needed quickly. The success of simplifying processes, reducing systems through the HRMS harmonization effort, and the new portal environment found that over 80 per cent of their HR inquiries were now being resolved in the first interaction. In addition to meeting the end-users' needs more efficiently, executives and manager had the data they needed in a single location for workforce-related decision making.

Endnotes

1 Sapient Insights, 2020–2021 HR Systems Survey White Paper, 23rd Annual Edition

2 Sapient Insights (formerly Sierra-Cedar Research) Global Employee and Manager Self Service Study, 2018

07

Time management applications

Introduction

At 16 I started working as a waitress for a small family restaurant about a mile from our home. A time capsule of Middle America, it reigned supreme in our little corner of the world as a comfortable spot for town gossip, endless cups of coffee and all-you-can eat fish on Fridays. Passing the cigarette vending machine through its heavy weighted front door felt a bit like stepping back in time, with its vinyl red booths, individual jukeboxes and U-shaped, yellow speckled Formica counter that was home to a frequent flow of truck drivers, local farmers and highway patrolmen. Most of the waitresses and short-order cooks worked in the restaurant for years and in return it allowed them schedules that fitted their family needs. These employees were a primary draw to the little restaurant – they knew without asking that Sara needed decaf, exactly how George liked his eggs cooked, and which Evans children needed constant distraction to allow the parents time to eat. They were highly skilled employees who worked like a well-oiled machine – breakfast and gossip were dished out in a timely matter, and tables were turned at a pace that would boggle the mind.

Us 'youngsters' – the term affectionately given to new employees by staff and long-time customers – paid our dues by working the slowest hours of the day or taking the nightshift, filled with a steady stream of one-time-visiting late-night travellers and the 3am bar closing crowd that had us questioning humanity but usually meant a decent night of tips and great stories to tell everyone the next day. We also worked the busy day and morning shifts, but we were tasked with cleaning bathrooms and break rooms and filling condiments – unpleasant but important tasks allowing us to slowly learn the customers and the business of working in a restaurant. This onboarding time was not fun, but everyone who stuck it out realized it was a great way to learn, train slowly and get to know the restaurant. It was an unspoken hiring process that made the restaurant run smoothly and probably looked terrible on paper because the lower-paid and younger workers had the fewest hours on the schedule.

It was in this environment that I learned the importance of time management applications, those tools that were used to track time and schedule shifts, enter days off or manage absences. When I started at the restaurant, everything was done manually by the store manager. Each night we would write in pencil on a little lined sheet of paper what time we started our shift and what time we ended, or how many breaks we took during our shift. Before Sunday of every week, all 36 employees were expected to fill out a handwritten sheet with the hours and days we could work, and the store manager would spend all day Monday locked away in his little back office, with copious amounts of pie and soda, manually building a schedule for the following weeks and entering our time sheets for the past weeks. It was not the most efficient process – there was always a mistake or two on some pay cheques that had to be adjusted, and newbies had to visit the store every Thursday to see if they were working that weekend. There were always a few unhappy employees – someone who could not get the days off they needed, or waitresses with too few or too many hours – but generally the staff was happy. The manager knew his staff and worked hard to meet their needs.

I worked at the restaurant all through high school and into the first few years of college, a great place that allowed time for studying, with good tips and a flexible schedule. In my last few years, I was no longer the 'youngster'; now a long-standing waitress with years of seniority, I pretty much always got the schedule I needed. In my sixth year, our little restaurant was bought by a corporate entity. At first it was just a name and menu change, but within a month we were introduced to the new time and attendance and scheduling software. The manager was being reassigned and the software and corporate would now be in charge of building our schedules and approving time worked. Our little corner of the world was changing – not only would we be entering our hours in a small computer in the back office, but our schedules would be posted weekly online. It sounded good, but there were some real issues in not having someone who understood the restaurant and the employees, or even a human being to discuss the implications of mistakes or changes to our pay cheques or schedules. Within a few weeks of the new application being rolled out the restaurant was in uproar. Although Sandy, who had worked at the restaurant for 15 years, had put in for all morning hours, the application scheduled her for several evening shifts when she had no babysitters available. Carol, who had worked mornings at the restaurant for over 30 years, was being asked to work fewer hours, cutting her benefits options and making it impossible to get her healthcare. Short-order cooks were being forced to take breaks during the busiest shifts, or work split days, coming in mornings and nights, with no one scheduled in between to prep and clean. The 'youngsters' were scattered throughout the schedule, without the necessary preparation or learning time – they were slowing down morning rushes and frustrating long-time customers. It was a disaster. And for me, well, I could no longer get the shifts I needed to work between my college classes and eventually left. Over time more long-time employees continued to leave and within five years our beloved little restaurant on the hill was unrecognizable and was soon out of business. The HR application and policies were not the only thing to blame for the restaurant's demise, but they were definitely part of the problem.

A somewhat drastic example, it is also a very real example of the impact that a poorly configured and poorly implemented time management application can have on any business, but particularly in those industries where optimizing time and the needs of your talent are always being balanced. These applications touch everyone in your organization, and in many cases make or break an organization's ability to keep critical talent.

The definitions

The primary function of time management systems in a work environment is to help an organization manage its vision of how work will be accomplished and achieve the organization's desired outcomes. These applications are sometimes called workforce management or labour management applications, but for the purposes of this book they are identified as time management or time solutions.

As seen in Figure 7.1, these applications help to organize and schedule the amount of time that a series of work activities should take an employee and to track the actual time spent. The applications are generally a mixture of administrative software used to design schedules and forecast workforce needs, and hardware and employee-facing software needed to track the actual location of the workforce completing the work, the activities they have completed and the timeframe in which it was all accomplished. They also often include applications that track the absence of workers or those on leave as well as providing a total view of the available workforce.

Although it might feel like the Human Resources function is the most logical owner for this category of HR Technology, 60 per cent of the time we see time management processes and applications managed by an organization's operations function,[1] particularly in industries like professional services, manufacturing, retail and healthcare, with multiple shifts and wide ranges of salaried and hourly workforces. In these environments operations is ultimately responsible for the cost of labour required to achieve their goals. Operations often buys, administers and oversees the applications' use – while Human Resources focuses on ensuring configurations for various regulations.

One of the reasons these applications are so important and managed so carefully is that they often ensure organizations are adhering to the wide range of regulations, which can differ by region, country and even city in some cases. When used appropriately these applications can provide guard rails for organizations with global workforces,

FIGURE 7.1 Time management applications category

ensuring organizations are aware if employees are working over the hours approved in a timeframe, in locations they may not be cleared to work due to training or security clearance, or in timeframes not allowed legally due to their age.

The complexity of the application required by an organization depends greatly on several factors:

- workforce types (hourly, salary, part-time, gig workers, contract workers);

- work environments (multi-location, safety issues, security issues, mobility, oversight);
- hours worked (multiple shifts, overtime, non-traditional work hours, fatigue concerns);
- regulations and agreements (younger workforces, older workforces, global requirements, negotiated labour contracts);
- type of work (physical requirements, skills requirements, knowledge requirements, expected customer interactions, expected use of technology, expected teamwork, leadership roles).

Time management systems are all about tracking how and where we spend our time at work, and ensuring we have the resources and skills needed to accomplish that work. They oversee what time and tasks are considered most valuable to an organization and support the planning, assignment and scheduling required to accomplish that work. The applications that fall under a time management solution should do more than just track and optimize work; on a practical level these applications ensure that employees are paid fairly for the time spent on work activities and ensure that an organization is compliant with all local and regional labour laws. They should also ensure an organization is safe, ethical and innovative in managing both resources and their activities.

The industry is fairly clear on the individual applications that traditionally fall into this HR systems category.

Time and attendance applications

Timekeeping systems that use a mixture of software and hardware to capture the location and time of work. Hourly workforces are more likely to use a digital timeclock or input device to track the exact hours worked. Salaried employees are more likely to enter their time in an employee self-service environment once or twice a week, or the company presets their work hours as they are generally ineligible for overtime depending on the region. With the onset of mobile technology, we are seeing more use of wearable devices for tracking work time as well. Some applications track both time and tasks for billable work environments or environments where pay is dependent on the work being done at any given moment.

Absence management applications

Software that tracks an employee's absence during expected work hours, due to illness, vacation or other unforeseen issues. These applications vary greatly by industry and the complexity of an organization's absence policies. Office workers may need to note when they are absent but may not need an additional headcount to fill in for their work. An absence in a manufacturing or retail environment requires a replacement employee is found as soon as possible to keep a business running. These applications also track the number of absent days against parameters set by the organization and additional requested time off. Generally, these are back-office applications, but they may have an employee screen for notifying the organization of an absence.

Leave management applications

These are sometimes purchased as part of an absence management application but are often part of outsourcing agreements as well and purchased separately. These applications definitely have an employee-facing environment, where employees can request both long- and short-term timeframes for leave. These systems often trigger a series of workflows needed to gain approval for the leave, steps required to fill the position if needed, and any policy assessment or legal paperwork required for longer leave requests. If paid time off is offered, the system may calculate accrued vacation time and compensation provided to absent employees.

Labour or workforce scheduling applications

These applications are specifically used when an organization needs to create and maintain a schedule for work that needs to be completed.

These are most often implemented for hourly workforces but can also be used as part of project management efforts, billable work, contract work or skills-based work. These applications build a schedule based on parameters set within the system, local labour requirements and outcomes an organization plans to achieve. Many applications also leverage machine learning to assess past time and attendance data to automatically build schedules for current work environments. These applications can build tremendous efficiencies and optimization, but as we noted in the introduction to the chapter, they can also miss important human elements to scheduling requirements and should be managed carefully. Newer applications are providing more autonomy to the employees themselves to request specific work times, swap shifts and build their own schedules within organizational parameters. These applications make the schedules accessible to the workforce and generally have tools for adjusting or making changes based on absence or leave inputs.

Labour or workforce budgeting applications

These applications are used to track current workforce numbers and to calculate the number of labour hours needed to produce the outcomes desired by the organization. They also generally have forecasting capabilities that allow an organization to see how adjustments in workforce numbers or location may impact expected outcomes. Sometimes these applications are part of the scheduling applications or an enterprise business planning application, but there are many industry-specific stand-alone tools for industries such as construction, manufacturing, retail and healthcare that also include industry-specific standards, impact of local regulations, details on required certifications and location differentiators that are important in budgeting exercises.

Time and attendance, absence management and leave management are the most widely adopted time management applications, with over 60 per cent of Sapient Insights' 23rd Annual HR Systems Survey respondents using all three of them, as noted in Figure 7.2. We are

FIGURE 7.2 Time management application adoption data, 2020

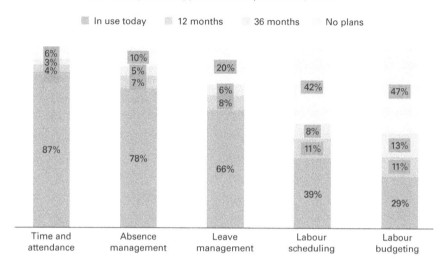

also seeing increased adoption of absence and leave management by organizations in all industries, due to increased global regulations concerning time worked and employee health and family needs, elevated during the 2020 COVID-19 pandemic. Labour scheduling and budgeting applications are complex solutions built to manage the operational workflow of specific organization types and are thus less likely to be adopted today.

The history of time and workforce management applications

In previous years, time management solutions were primarily adopted by organizations with large hourly and part-time workforces such as in retail, manufacturing and healthcare. Today, we are seeing adoption levels increase in all of these application areas as organizations have greater need to track time and work activities for highly skilled workforces, in addition to managing complex leave, absence and scheduling regulations around the globe.

Over the years, we have also seen changes in how organizations are selecting and purchasing time management applications and integrating them with existing applications. Today, 28 per cent of organizations are using a time management application that is offered as a module of their enterprise resource application, such as Oracle Cloud ERP, Workday or Infor ERP, and 31 per cent are using a time management application that is offered as a module of their human capital suite, such as UKG Pro (UltiPro), Ceridian Dayforce or Paycor. Just 40 per cent of organizations have purchased their time management application as a point solution, such as UKG Dimension (Kronos) or WorkForce Software, down almost 40 per cent since 2014.[2]

It is also important to note that many organizations have made heavy investments in their on-premise time management solutions and traditional time clocks that make it difficult to quickly change these applications or to move to more engaging cloud-based applications. Organizations are beginning to see the advantages of moving to more mobile-friendly solutions with reduced replacement costs, particularly as a result of events in 2020 when tracking location and work groups became life and death discussions for many employees.

Many organizations are also trying to adjust their time tracking and scheduling applications to adjust to expectations and regulations concerning issues of employee data privacy, health and safety issues, the relationship between work optimization efforts and socioeconomic concerns, and increased expectations for work–life balance options for everyone.

Why you need to care

Although I had a clear understanding of the impact of time management applications from my work at the restaurant, I was too young then to realize that it was not the software at the time but the way it was applied that caused our little restaurant to change so rapidly. It was not until I was asked to work with the operations team for a large retail organization that I came to understand how central time management applications were to all other areas of HR and the impact they could have on employee engagement and company outcomes.

My experience was that HR primarily viewed the time management systems as an extension of the time clocks – but to the operations teams, this technology was a critical tool in their ability to meet quotas, increase margins and communicate with their workforce. It was their primary connection to employees, from the corporate offices to distribution centres and retail environments. It gave them a daily touch point with every employee in the organization. It was this system that highlighted for them when an employee was dealing with a difficult situation at home or when a work environment was becoming too stressful. It provided a venue to push daily messages and gave managers data on where they needed to hire or increase training. It was data from this environment that drove most of their requests for HR intervention. Run separately with an operations focus, time management solutions can definitely help an organization stay in compliance and run efficiently.

When time management is elevated from a transactional system to the same strategic level of importance as an organization's talent management solution, HR immediately has the tools to optimize both the work and the talent within an organization and to quickly adjust to changing external factors. When organizations combine these solutions with powerful business intelligence and analytics tools, the outcomes are impressive. Research has shown that organizations that leverage a suite of time management applications with data integrated into the broader HR system and business planning environments were regularly correlated with HR organizations that were viewed as more strategic and had continuously higher HR and talent outcomes.[3]

This finding brought some clarity to another issue that we've struggled with for several years in the HR community: finding the real business impact of talent management solutions. It is easy to show indirect cost savings and improved engagement metrics when implementing talent management solutions, but these are often less relevant to business leaders. It is the combination of talent management and time management data that turns the conversation from an HR discussion to a strategic operations discussion.

Even if you are an organization that does not track time on an hourly or daily basis for your employees, there are systems and people in your organization that assign projects, pass out duties and assess the work conducted. Microsoft Office and Google have both launched platforms and tools that track employee activity, performance and even engagement based on the time spent in their products or assigned through their calendar applications. Even if you are not using a traditional time management application, your organization is managing this workflow in some way with existing tools and processes, and every organization will need to consider how, when and where that data can be used to make decisions that impact the employee and the organization.

HANDS-ON ACTIVITIES

- Identify the percentage of each workforce type managed as part of your total workforce base:
  - Exempt (salary)
  - Non-exempt (hourly)
  - Part-time
  - Gig workers
  - Contractors
- Identify the top two types of workforce managed by your organization (primary workforces).
- For each of your primary workforce types, identify which of these applications are in use as a stand-alone point solution application, part of your ERP suite or part of another HR suite, or not in use at all.

TABLE 7.1

Time management applications	Application use and deployment mode			
	Not in use	ERP suite	HR suite	Point solution
Time and attendance				
Absence management				
Leave management				
Labour/workforce scheduling				
Labour/workforce budgeting				

- Describe the work environment for each primary workforce type.
- For each primary workforce type, identify how they access time-tracking and scheduling applications:
  - Time clock
  - Computer
  - Kiosk
  - Mobile
  - Wearable
  - Other
- Assess the current level of satisfaction your two primary workforces and managers have with these tools/processes for workforce time management on a scale of 1 (terrible) to 5 (excellent) – this can be assessed through discussion, interviews, surveys or your personal observations.

Workforce user experience:

- Clocking in or clocking out
- Accessing schedules
- Requesting time off
- Requesting schedule changes/swapping shifts

Manager's/supervisor's user experience:

- Adjusting inaccurate clock-ins or clock-outs
- Creating schedules
- Communicating schedules
- Approving requests for time off or shift swaps
- Viewing scheduling risks via overtime, regulations or employee frustrations

CASE STUDY

The human side of workforce time management

The retail associates are the heart and soul of the Macy's enterprise. They are the front-line employees with whom customers interact and they can make or break a customer's purchasing decision. One of Macy's' main goals is to build and retain a quality talent pool, which is difficult due to the high turnover found in retail. The turnover for hourly employees can be as high as 65 per cent, with the cost of replacing them around $1,000 per employee. In the past decade, Macy's has been on a journey to get to the root cause of the high turnover and why employees are leaving.

The team at Macy's learned about four universal retail workforce truths:

- *Consumer expectations are changing.* Customer experiences matter while at the same time retail is becoming more expensive to staff (increases in minimum wage and local regulations).

- *Engaged associates produce more outstanding results.* Associates need to be shopper advocates and make the in-store experience more compelling.

- *Turnover is constant.* Over half of the retail workforce has one foot out the door. Unengaged associates take more sick days, give little effort, miss deadlines, have poor sales, etc.

- *There has been dramatic change.* Workforce demographics are shifting. Baby Boomers, Gen X, millennials and Gen Z are all working together.

These truths apply to almost any retail organization, but Macy's wanted to create solutions to these potential problems. The company laid out the expectations that it had for every single retail employee, the first time it had tried something like this. Macy's leadership believed that engaged associates help build consumer loyalty and bolster sales, and they set clear expectations for an engaged employee's behaviours. By setting these expectations, it was able to weed out the disengaged employees very quickly: around 85 per cent of the disengaged workforce left immediately after the team presented the expectations. Once these employees had gone, the Macy's team shaped their workforce to connect with the shoppers on a new level. The team chose to turn to employee engagement software to guide the workforce. The new software allowed employees power over scheduling and freed managers to develop a customer service culture in their stores. This solution empowered associates and increased their engagement with the brand by changing the dynamic from them being told when they were working to choosing when they wanted to work. It also shows how technology and empowerment can come together to build a better and well-engaged workforce.[4,5]

Endnotes

1   Sapient Insights (Sierra-Cedar) 2018–2019 HR Systems Survey, 21st Annual Edition

2   Sapient Insights, 2020–2021 HR Systems Survey White Paper, 23rd Annual Edition

3   Sapient Insights (Sierra-Cedar), 2016–2017 Annual HR Systems Survey White Paper, 19th annual edition

4   Denman, T (2017) How Macy's Decreased Employee Turnover by 28%, *Retail Info Systems*, https://risnews.com/how-macys-decreased-employee-turnover-28 (archived at https://perma.cc/6QAR-72CF)

5   Berthiaume, D (2015) KronosWorks: Improving employee scheduling top retail priority, *Chain Store Age*, https://chainstoreage.com/operations/kronosworks-improving-employee-scheduling-top-retail-priority (archived at https://perma.cc/T2VR-E7LJ)

08

Talent management applications

Introduction

When I started working for a large national bank early in my career, one of the first things I learned was that there was a 'right type of customer'. Products, marketing efforts and employee talking points were all tailored for an extremely specific type of household with disposable income, brand new cars and a long-standing credit history. It was also clear that my family was not the right type of customer – we made do with a single income, had two used cars and two young boys, mountains of student loan debt and an almost non-existent credit history. In the banks' eyes there was not much room for a family that was starting out or just learning how to manage their finances.

Early forms of talent management programs were built on much the same premise: employees were either top performers and high potentials or they were not. Programs and incentives were designed to identify and motivate top performers and create a competitive environment among everyone else. Well, soon after leaving that job I started using a bank that had programs and tools that fit the needs of multiple clients, in every stage of financial readiness. They welcomed my young family, provided education and incentivized good financial habits. Within 10 years I had come a lot closer to the vision of the earlier bank's ideal customer but I have no intention of switching banks today. Similarly, current talent management practices for most organizations have evolved into a tailored employee experience that understands that everyone's career journey is unique and everyone is part of achieving the organization's business goals.

The category of talent management is a relatively new area of HR systems – supporting the HR practice areas that recruit, onboard, develop and manage performance of an organization's workforce. My HR career started in this domain area when I was a learning professional fresh out of graduate school filled with all the latest and greatest ideas for educating adults and improving performance. I quickly found out that real change would not come from training alone, it also required pay incentives, performance measures, skill alignment and employee engagement. If I wanted to effect real change in an organization I needed to get outside of my narrow focus on learning and look at what was really driving organizational behaviours and outcomes.

One of my first big projects that allowed me to do this was a skills and competency management program that took months to implement. Our team was asked to look at the entire lifecycle of a retail banking associate and help define the skills and competency levels of the most successful employees so that we could recruit, develop and assess performance based on these standard expectations. I spent months conducting a full job analysis, interviewing focus groups and business leaders, and conducting blind tested assessments with existing and new employees. We filled binders with long lists of knowledge and skillsets needed to successfully accomplish each task in the retail bank environment and then added guidelines for behaviours and levels of competency, to create a competency framework for each career path in retail banking. From these competency frameworks we built recruiting job descriptions, incentive plans, performance metrics and development programs to support employees who wanted to follow these well-defined career paths. It was a thing of beauty, two long years of work – and one of the greatest learning experiences of my early career. Within six months, our binders of skills and knowledge were outdated; within a year our competency models and frameworks were almost obsolete as retail banking roles shifted dramatically with the onset of online banking and new regulations.

This was my first lesson in one of the greatest challenges in addressing actual talent management – the world is always spinning, changing and innovating. We had the right concepts, but the wrong tools. We understood that defining the knowledge, skills, behaviours and motivators was important, but what we did not have was a mechanism for continuous update. Enter the era of the talent management application category and its focus on capturing skills, competencies, performance and training data from the employee's and manager's perspectives.

The definitions

The primary function of talent management applications is to help an organization manage its vision of talent in a way that achieves outcomes. Talent is a broad term that often gets used without a clear definition, but every organization has talent. Talent could be defined as critical skills, senior leaders, high potentials or the entire workforce – whichever population an organization has defined as critical to the survival, growth and/or strategy of the organization. The applications that fall under a talent management solution do more than just improve the processes and workflows of the employee lifecycle, they also ensure that an organization views every person as an individual, with a set of unique profile details, and, as seen in Figure 8.1, provide tools to help recruit, retain, develop, compensate, improve performance and grow careers in a way that acknowledges that profile. The industry is fairly clear on the individual applications that fall into this HR system category.

Recruiting and talent acquisition applications

A critical component of any talent management solution, this application or group of applications manages the recruiting process from job creation and posting to candidate sourcing, assessment and selection. There are three major audiences involved in the recruiting process who use these applications on a regular basis: HR recruiters, hiring managers and candidates.

FIGURE 8.1   Talent management applications category

The most prominent application in this category is the applicant tracking system, primarily focused on automating the process of opening a job requisition, defining the job role and allowing candidates to apply for that open position online. The application tracking system is particularly important in ensuring that organizations follow all the legal requirements mandated by local regulations in fair hiring practices and capturing new hire data needed for reporting to local regulatory entities.

In recent years, organizations have purchased additional modules or stand-alone applications that focus on managing the recruiting marketing process, the candidate relationship management process, and the interview, assessment and selection process. Many of these new applications are some of the earliest applications in the HR Technology space to adopt machine learning algorithms for ranking, rating and decision support tools.

Major issues impacting the recruiting and talent acquisition technology space include:

• the need to reduce systemic biases that exist in machine learning selection tools built on historical data;

• the need to address candidate data privacy requests while still complying with legal data reporting regulations;

• hiring standards that require experience versus cultural fits and learning capabilities (leaving entry-level candidates unable to move into critical job markets).

Recruiting technology often comes as separate modules that can be purchased as point solutions or as part of a recruiting suite or HR suite of applications.

Onboarding/mobility applications

This software manages the process and compliance tasks required when transitioning a job candidate into an employee. The most common use of these applications is to reduce administrative efforts by creating cross-organizational workflows for new employees that include everything from completing new hire paperwork to setting up security badges and computer access. Often there are also important cultural onboarding components that provide social connections to existing employees, learning content and a pre-designed set of tasks that help the employee feel more connected to the organization and quickly get up to speed in their new role. These applications are sometimes used when transitioning internal employees to new job roles.

Major issues impacting the onboarding technology space include:

- the need to address employee data privacy requests while still complying with legal data reporting regulations;
- work-from-home policies and standards, including hardware and software requirements.

Onboarding technology often comes as a separate module that can be purchased as a point solution or as part of a recruiting suite or HR suite of applications.

Performance management applications

Another critical component of a talent management solution, this software is designed to help organizations set employee performance goals, assess employee progress towards those goals, and record final outcomes and document a manager's or peer's reviews of the circumstances that had an impact on those outcomes. The primary audience throughout the year for these applications are managers and employees, and generally once or twice a year HR will conduct a performance review that rolls individual performance data into an enterprise view for senior leadership. Annual performance data is often used in calculating employee pay rises, bonuses or career opportunities.

Newer versions of these applications include features for conducting project assessments, task management, peer reviews, customer reviews and continuous performance management. We are also seeing a growing trend towards environmental data being used to assess employee performance, video monitoring, workforce productivity tools (Microsoft, Google), wearables and environmental sensors. The use of this data is very new, and currently these applications tend to focus on suggested performance improvements, but it is expected that this area of performance management will grow and require new levels of oversight and ethics.

Major issues impacting the performance management technology space include:

- the need to reduce systemic biases that exist in machine learning assessment tools built on historical data;
- the need to reduce bias in performance review language and ratings;
- the need to address employee data privacy requests while still complying with legal data reporting regulations.

Performance management technology is generally adopted as part of a talent or HR suite, although there are examples of point solutions still in the market.

Learning and development applications

One of the most critical components of a talent management solution, this application or group of applications generally supports all aspects of learning for an organization, including assessing learning needs, learning creation, learning access, organization of learning content, compliance tracking, performance support and management of the overall learning process. There are four major audiences involved in the learning process who use these applications on a regular basis: learning creators, learning administrators, learners and managers.

The most prominent application in this category is the learning management system, initially designed to support learning that was only needed and approved by the organization; the application provided access to self-paced learning and registration for instructor-led learning. The LMS also has robust reporting capabilities to provide clear documentation for compliance-based training requirements.

In recent years, organizations have purchased additional modules or stand-alone applications that focus on putting learning creation and selection in the hands of the learners, creating personalized learning experiences or providing work-embedded performance support.

Many of these new applications are some of the earliest applications in the HR Technology space to adopt emerging technology that uses machine learning and augmented reality to help support matching and expanding learning experiences.

Major issues impacting the learning and development technology space include:

• the need to reduce systemic biases that exist in machine learning used to select prescribed training, built on historical data;

• the need to address systemic biases that exist in learning content and learning language;

• the need to address employee data privacy requests while still complying with legal data reporting regulations.

Learning and development applications are most often purchased as part of a learning suite, talent suite or point solutions, with a growing number of organizations also adopting the learning application embedded in their HR suite of applications.

Compensation and rewards

This software helps organizations plan and administer employee monetary compensation packages, conduct pay analysis, set pay scales and develop salary structures. These applications need to be very flexible as they must utilize several sets of data points that come from other applications or externally to conduct their analysis work, including market salary survey data, employee performance data, employee location data, organization structure and job role definitions, and the organization's financial planning data. There are generally just two major audiences that are involved in the compensation and rewards application on a regular basis: compensation analysts and sometimes managers for approval screens.

Newer versions of these applications include scenario planning tools, specialized market surveying capabilities, and the creation and publication of total reward statements for employees. Total rewards reporting often combines monetary (bonuses, raises, commission) and non-monetary (retirement, benefits, perks) information.

Major issues impacting the compensation and rewards technology space include:

- the need to remove pay equity gaps for similar work across all employees, no matter their race, gender, age or other protected demographics;
- the need to assess work based on skills utilized versus job role titles;
- increasing demands for pay transparency and full disclosures.

Compensation and reward applications are often purchased as stand-alone applications but are also just as often purchased as a module in a talent suite or an HR suite.

Succession and career management

This software is generally a mirror set of applications that focus on both the organization and the employee as two parts of the talent management conversation. In the succession planning category, the focus is on the organization's needs, categorizing leadership roles, assessing employee readiness to move into those roles, and assessing gaps in skills, experience or knowledge that need to be addressed before employees can replace specific leaders. On the career management side of these applications the focus is on the employee's needs, assessing an employee's current and future capabilities, possible career paths that match their capabilities and personal goals, and ways for the employee to fill the gaps in skills, experience and knowledge required for those career paths. These are complex applications that require a large amount of input from HR, employees, managers and senior leadership, which makes them hard to populate and often harder to maintain. Newer versions of the application often include coaching and mentoring solutions, internal mobility jobs or gig matching, peer reward and recommendations, and personal assessment tools.

Major issues impacting the succession and career management technology space include:

- the need to reduce systemic biases that exist in machine learning succession ranking and rating tools built on historical data;
- the need to reduce systemic biases that exist in machine learning career recommendation tools built on historical data;
- the need to address employee data privacy requests while still complying with legal data reporting regulations.

Succession and career management applications are most often purchased as part of a talent management suite, although there are examples of point solutions still in the market.

Skills and competency management

This software is an evolving market, originally the basis of most talent management solutions as a basic employee profile that catalogued the skills, experiences and knowledge that were most important to achieving an organization's defined goals. In recent years more emphasis has been placed on applications that help organizations create a full picture of their skills and competency requirements, set up unique organizational skills taxonomies (categorization, organization, relationships), and assign skills and competency levels to job roles and employees for the purpose of conducting skills-based talent management. These applications often have assessments for skills gap analysis and forecasting tools for future skills requirements.

Although the terms 'skills' and 'competencies' are often used interchangeably in terms of talent management, it is important to understand the distinct differences as these are fundamental to an organization's approach to talent management.

Skills refer to a specific learned ability to do something well. This may include the knowledge or experience required to gain that skill as part of the definition. Organizations usually have hard skills, soft skills and sometimes certified skills. Skills can be learned quickly, usually with a clear set of knowledge and experience.

Example: Mary has the skill to play the piano.

Example: Mary has good verbal communication skills.

Competencies are a person's knowledge, behaviours or abilities that are needed to be successful in a specific function or job role. Competencies are generally developed over time and include multiple and diverse sets of skills, knowledge and experiences.

Example: Mary has the competency to lead the band.

Example: Mary has the ability to communicate with all levels of the organization.

Major issues impacting the skills and competency management technology space include:

- the need for constant updating, maintenance and validation of skills and competency data sets;
- the need to reduce systemic biases that exist in machine learning skills-matching tools built on historical data;
- the need to reduce system biases that exist in skills databases built on historical data;
- the need to address employee data privacy requests while still complying with legal data reporting regulations.

Skills and competency management applications are highly technical solutions that are often adopted as part of an HR or talent suite or may be purchased as a stand-alone solution, but they always require deep process-level integration with other HR applications to create value and keep up with the rapidly changing requirements of the organization.

These applications are tightly connected to a workforce's ability to grow, innovate and achieve HR and business outcomes. As seen in Figure 8.2, recruiting applications have the highest levels of adoption in the talent management category, with 86 per cent of organizations using some form of recruiting technology to attract and hire new

FIGURE 8.2   Talent management applications, adoption data 2020

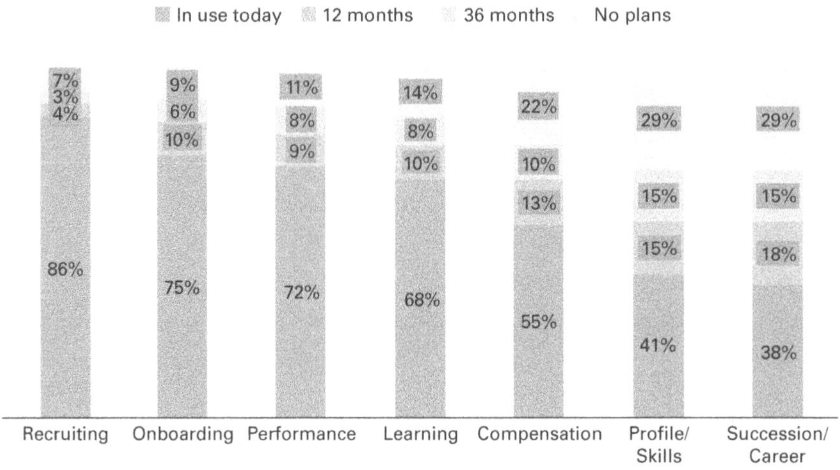

employees while just 38 per cent of organizations have adopted a succession and career management application.[1] This unequal level of adoption shows a real issue in the talent management category, where investment in recruiting and hiring new talent often overshadows investment in retaining and developing talent.

The history of talent management applications

The origins of the term talent management are generally attributed to a 1997 McKinsey & Company study on the importance of strategic HR and a subsequent paper on the topic in 1998.[2] Coincidentally, 1997 was also the first year that the Hunter Group would release survey findings on the new phenomenon of HR self-service applications, which would note that new HRIS self-service functionality would require a commitment to a new way of doing business – for example, to support talent management, it would be necessary for employees themselves to provide up-to-date information on their knowledge, skills and aptitudes.[3]

In economic terms, the late 1990s was a time of job growth and business opportunities. For the first time in years there were more jobs than available skilled workers, and the relationship between employee and employer was being rapidly redefined in terms of supply and demand. As competition for skilled knowledge workers heated up, organizations needed to offer new benefits, experiences and opportunities. Even with all these new opportunities, however, it quickly became apparent that organizations were losing skilled workers as fast as they were bringing them in the door. Employees now had 24/7 access to the internet and brand-new online job boards which were putting fresh job opportunities literally at their fingertips. Nothing epitomized this concept as much as the 1999 US Super Bowl XXXIII commercial from Monster.com, 'When I grow up …', featuring children aspirationally talking about future jobs that sarcastically came a little too close to the reality of the viewers' current job environment, pointing out that no one dreamed of filing all day or dealing with miserable bosses when they grew up.[4] After that commercial, Monster.com grew to become one of the largest job boards in the market before industry consolidation and an economic downturn reduced its competitive advantage. Culturally there was also a major backlash from a new generation of workers who had grown up in the 1970s and 1980s, watching their parents caught up in rounds of employment reductions as companies optimized work through outsourcing and automation and middle-management reduction practices. This generation of workers were left with a bitter view of organizational loyalty and trust.

It was in this environment that the talent management applications were born, a newer and cooler online version of the early on-premise HRIS modules that were used only for administering training data, recruiting paperwork and pay rise information. These applications were some of the first cloud-based enterprise applications, generally with a single line of code and continuous-update models. The primary user was no longer assumed to be an HR or learning administrator but the employee themselves. Administrators still had their admin screens for setup, configuration and maintenance, but there was no option to turn employee screens on or off, they just existed and were part of the new software.

Being internet-based businesses also meant that these technology vendors could enter the space rather quickly, with a much smaller investment than their larger competitors. At one time the domain of software development belonged to only the largest companies, like IBM, SAP or ADP; in the era of the dotcom boom, any small team with access to the internet and a few savvy programmers could begin to build business software, and they did. Initially these applications were stand-alone point solutions focused on individual niches: learning, performance, recruiting, skills management. As these vendors matured and grew in the early 2000s they needed to keep existing customers and grow market share, so they started to add talent-focused modules to their original offerings.

For example, in 2005 Cornerstone OnDemand changed its original name from CyberU, re-platformed and added a performance management module. I remember this clearly because I was buying an LMS that year for my large retail organization. I was frustrated that none of the vendors in our search was embracing this new concept of talent management and I asked my intern that year to conduct an online search for the newest LMSs in the market: she brought me CyberU. She proudly informed me that they were actually tracking learning and performance in the same system, so we could connect our performance reviews, individual learning plans and content in a seamless process for our employees. It was such a novel idea, and just what I had been looking for in our search, but that was the only cloud-based option on my list. I asked them to fly out from California to our Ohio headquarters for our demo, and although I really liked what they were offering, I thought my very conservative retail organization would probably select one of the more traditional applications. In a conference room with our head of HR, head of learning, head of compliance and safety, CIO, and VP of operations, CyberU informed us they were changing their name to Cornerstone OnDemand and commenced to blow the competition out of the water as they demonstrated a fully online learning and performance platform, with an interface optimized for end-users. It took me another year to fully fund the project, and by then the talent management market had taken off.

By 2007 the term integrated talent management was being extensively used in marketing materials for these applications, with a heavy focus on the employee experience from recruiting to retirement, as seen in Figure 8.3.[5]

For about 10 years these applications dominated the HR Technology landscape, with organizations snapping them up as they envisaged engaged employees and managers happily using these applications, filling them with all the data needed to strategically recruit, assess and develop this more demanding workforce. As cloud applications, they also required no major signoff from CIOs and IT staff to purchase hardware or manage lengthy implementations. The new online pricing models were pay-as-you-go subscriptions instead of hefty investments in software code, allowing organizations to make smaller upfront investments and decrease overall risk. At the same time HRMS, time management and payroll applications were still on-premise administrative applications that were hard to use and organizations had invested large sums of money in recent years to implement these applications, which meant replacements were unlikely. Organizations bought the talent management suites to be their front-end employee experience and figured out every way possible to transfer data between

FIGURE 8.3   An integrated talent management model

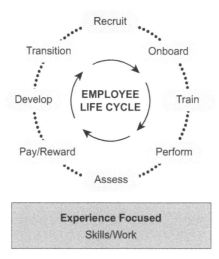

these administrative and talent applications, including weekly flat file updates, manual Excel spreadsheet entries or actually building custom-coded integrations. By 2015, 55 per cent of organizations noted that they had a talent management suite in use.[6]

The old adage 'if you can't beat them join them' is a perfect explanation of what happened in the late 2010s as a frenzy of acquisitions in the HR Technology space changed the landscape for ever. Larger talent suites were purchasing smaller niche applications to fill out the full talent management offering – for example, no fewer than 10 acquisitions and divestitures were part of the creation of one of the largest talent management suites of the era, SumTotal Systems, until it was acquired by Skillsoft in 2014. At the same time ERP and HRMS solutions were on a buying spree, kicked off in 2010 when SAP agreed to purchase SuccessFactors, one of the most successful talent suites to grow out of the performance management space, and then Oracle purchased Taleo, a talent suite that had the largest number of users in the recruiting market.

As great as acquisitions are for quickly gaining market share, talent and existing customers, they also require a great deal of time to effectively merge two cultures, different technology platforms and customer service models. While these organizations were addressing internal acquisition efforts over new customer requirements, it made room for several large HRMS and ERP providers such as Workday

FIGURE 8.4 Prepare to deal with continuous acquisition and merger activity in this space

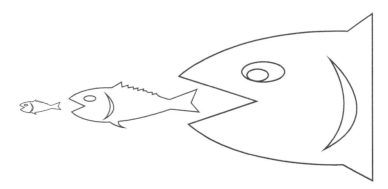

and Ultimate Software time to focus on building out their talent management capabilities organically. We should note that these organizations did acquire some smaller applications and teams in their building process, but not to the extent of the larger platforms – and their more streamlined and integrated applications saw dramatic growth during this time in the use of their performance, learning and recruiting modules even if the talent applications were not as fully matured as the acquired organizations' applications.

You may be wondering why you need to understand this confusing and messy background of the talent suite, especially if today we are seeing more organizations purchase their talent applications as modules within their HRMS or once again as point solutions. First off, if your organization is more than a few years old, it is highly likely that your existing HR systems environment includes one or more of these legacy applications, along with a large amount of custom integration code, even if everything is technically being licensed or subscribed to from the same vendor. Knowing an application's history can provide great context for understanding its strengths and weaknesses, along with where the data sits and how easy it is to access.

Additionally, HR Technology application businesses, like any other business environment, have cycles, and if you stay in the industry for any length of time you will likely see several cycles of the growth of point solutions, a series of mergers and acquisitions to a suite of applications, followed by more mergers and acquisitions among the largest platform providers, followed by the regrowth of point solutions. Understanding that change is constant can help reduce frustration with current technology environments, especially when you know it is a point in time, and also ensures that organizations make reasonable HR Technology investment decisions, knowing that the industry is in constant motion.

Why you need to care

In order to stay competitive and attract a workforce that is passionate and motivated, organizations have begun to redirect the HR conversation from compliance and risk to one of experience and outcomes. Today's workforce demands more personal attention; they understand the value of their personal knowledge and skills, and they thrive on opportunities to grow and increase their experiences. Employees are looking for roles that allow them to blend their personal goals with their professional careers, and organizations that tap into these new expectations and change their approach to human capital management will find an amazing new resource in their employees. Understanding this new workforce and how to harness its enthusiasm becomes a critical requirement for organizations that hope to achieve outcomes and growth.

The business of HR is always about achieving outcomes. How we achieve those outcomes makes all the difference. The last few years, particularly 2020, brought into sharp focus just how diverse we are when it comes to achieving business outcomes and meeting the needs of our employees. During the global healthcare crisis and economic downturn, we saw major business and talent crisis by industry: healthcare and grocery stores saw rapidly increasing workloads for front-line employees, while travel and entertainment industries furloughed thousands of field employees overnight as businesses closed for undetermined amounts of time.

Some organizations managed the crisis focused only on the bottom line, choosing to keep workers in possibly unsafe environments or rushing layoffs without proper communications. Other organizations chose to gather data, focus on safety, make leadership-level sacrifices, have clear communication during workforce reductions, use their talent information, and innovate and change where possible. The number one response to the healthcare crisis in almost every industry and region was redistribution of an organization's critical workforce[7] – making the work of HR and talent management a key factor in the survival of almost every impacted organization. Organizations that entered the healthcare crisis with a clear understanding of their workforce's capabilities were simply better prepared to pivot; the huge investment organizations had been making in talent management and data capturing efforts paid all its dues in that crisis alone.

Looking forward, as talent management applications continue to mature in all areas, skills-based management is the future of this industry. If you recall, I started my career over 20 years ago realizing the power and impact of skills-based management but also quickly found the tools were unable to keep up with the pace of change. Since the data required for this level of management must come from the individual employee working on the job, employees and managers alike have been clear that entering the additional data needed for this kind of management requires more personal value for the individual themselves. With the emergence of machine learning, environmental data gathering and 24/7 access to workers through mobile devices, we are beginning to see the possibilities of how skills-based management can be accomplished with less intrusion and heavy lifting.

Skills-based management is the shift from managing the workforce by standard, defined job roles to management of a critical set of skills that each employee possesses and allocating those skills in a way that benefits both the employee and the organization. The old mantra of right person, right place, right time assumes that there is a single job and singe place that everyone fits, rather than a series of work experiences that develops the employee and supports the needs of the business at any given time. A more fluid work model can be accommodated only with a skills-based management model – something that is not yet supported by the existing technology. The healthcare crisis put a spotlight on this when 65 per cent of organizations that needed to assign workers based on skills versus job roles simply did not have up-to-date information available to make those critical talent decisions.[8] As you work through these critical issues in your organization, keeping a close eye on the current and future talent management applications will ensure that you can help your organization stay ahead of the curve in this conversation.

In the midst of these conversations every HR professional needs to be well versed on changing regulations and public perception on the topics of bias, institutional racism, data privacy, data governance and data security. These are particularly important in the case of talent management applications as these applications are assigning value to information and making decisions about where people work and how valuable that work is for the organization. Leaving too much decision making in the hands of the technology is just as dangerous as allowing every employee to make those decisions without company guidance.

EXAMPLE

In January of 2021 HireVue, a video interview and assessment vendor, announced that it had removed the facial analysis component from its screening assessments as concerns about the transparent and appropriate use of artificial intelligence in employment decisions grow.[9] The controversial feature used algorithms to assign certain traits and qualities to job applicants' facial expressions in video interviews and came under fire when the Electronic Privacy Information Centre (EPIC) filed an official complaint to the US Federal Trade Commission to investigate HireVue's business practices.[10]

These topics will be discussed in more detail in the emerging technology section of the book, but it is well worth noting that organizations and leaders are held accountable for their decisions even if they used a technology to help them make those decisions.

Selecting and purchasing a talent management application often aligns with a specific operational request, such as the need for rapid hiring or new training requirements, but when the data and processes in these systems are combined with other HR application areas we've already discussed, such as benefits, time management or service delivery, they can work hand in hand to help organizations balance the need to gather data, assign the actual work and achieve the desired performance. They can also help fulfil individual employee aspirations that often are left out of the equation. When managed with transparency and ethical use of data talent management applications can be tightly connected to organizational outcomes, employee culture and employee engagement.

HANDS-ON ACTIVITIES

- Identify which of these applications are in use in your organization and whether they are part of a suite of technologies, a point solution or not in use at all.

TABLE 8.1

Talent applications	Application use and deployment model				
	Not in use	ERP suite	HR suite	Talent suite	Point solution
Recruiting and talent acquisition					
Onboarding and mobility					
Performance management					
Learning and development					
Compensation and rewards					
Succession and career management					
Skills and competency management					

- Review the talent management processes for each of these workforce categories and identify whether the talent management experience for them is the same, somewhat different or very different from your own experience.

- For each category that has a 'very different' experience, what do you believe is the primary reason for their vastly different experience provided by the organization?

- Describe the primary way your organization creates and maintains job descriptions. How often are they updated?

- Describe the primary way the organization tracks and maintains its knowledge of the skills and competencies of its existing employees. How often is this updated?

TABLE 8.2

Talent applications	Application use and deployment model					
	Executives	Managers/ Supervisors	HQ office employees	Non-HQ office employees	Field/ Retail employees	Others
Recruiting and talent acquisition						
Onboarding and mobility						
Performance management						
Learning and development						
Compensation and rewards						
Succession and career management						
Skills and competency management						

- Does your organization have a process for supporting internal mobility? If yes, describe the process and tools. If no, interview your HR and IT teams to identify why this process does not exist.

THE HUMAN SIDE OF WORKFORCE TALENT MANAGEMENT

When organizations face cataclysmic events, as many did in 2020, with the challenges of a global pandemic, rapid economic shifts, and major social justice movements all in the same year - it is an organizations talent that can be the difference between simply surviving versus prospering. When externally an organization sees nothing but barriers to success, the ability to look inward and harness internal talent can turn challenges into opportunities.

While the COVID-19 crisis dramatically impacted many industries, higher education faced stronger headwinds than most. San Jacinto Community College was the exception in the crowded field of struggling colleges, an institution that has been able to take the pandemic in stride thanks to its pre-pandemic investments in HR and Talent technology. With over 2,000 employees, the college is devoted to promoting student success, academic progress, university transfer, and employment in the local community.

While San Jacinto knew that offering digital tools and services was non-negotiable for students, the college also saw an opportunity to innovate for its faculty and staff. In 2016, the college adopted Cornerstone's suit of Talent Management tools for recruiting, learning, performance, and career development, a broad sweep of functionality. By digitizing these areas of the college's operations before the COVID-19 crisis, San Jacinto was able to improve processes, effectively transition its staff to remote work, and provide learning and development resources that made the transition easier for faculty. And as a result, the college was able to continue – rather than delay – its growth path during 2020. San Jacinto Community College continues to look for new ways to innovate its operations to stay relevant amid an increasingly digital environment. Offering more online classes with more flexible learning options and prepared teachers has increased accessibility for students – helping the college stay committed to its mission of promoting student success.

Endnotes

1 Sapient Insights, 2020–2021 HR Systems Survey White Paper, 23rd Annual Edition

2 Chambers, EG, Foulon, M, Handfield-Jones, H and Hankin, SM (1998) The war for talent, *McKinsey Quarterly*, 3 (3), 44–57

3 The Hunter Group, Human Resources Self Service: One Year Later – 1997

4 Monster.com (nd) 'When I grow up' commercial, *YouTube*, www.youtube.com/watch?v=myG8hq1Mk00 (archived at https://perma.cc/2TY9-MZ58)

5 Sapient Insights, 2020–2021 HR Systems Survey White Paper, 23rd Annual Edition

6 Sapient Insights (Sierra-Cedar), 2014–2015 HR Systems Survey, 17th Annual Edition

7 Sapient Insights, 2020–2021 HR Systems Survey White Paper, 23rd Annual Edition

8 Sapient Insights, 2020–2021 HR Systems Survey White Paper, 23rd Annual Edition

9 Maurer, R (2021) HireVue discontinues facial analysis screening, *SHRM*, www.shrm.org/resourcesandtools/hr-topics/talent-acquisition/pages/hirevue-discontinues-facial-analysis-screening.aspx (archived at https://perma.cc/LN7S-KN9T)

10 Harwell, D (2019) Rights group files federal complaint against AI-hiring firm HireVue, citing 'unfair and deceptive' practices, *The Washington Post*, www.washingtonpost.com/technology/2019/11/06/prominent-rights-group-files-federal-complaint-against-ai-hiring-firm-hirevue-citing-unfair-deceptive-practices/ (archived at https://perma.cc/F8D5-8CQK)

09

HR analytics and planning

Introduction

If you think back to your first experience with HR in any job role, it probably included a request for information – from submitting your CV to completing new-hire paperwork, every interaction was a transfer of data. Sometimes sharing that data was beneficial to you personally, but often it felt as though your data was lost down a deep, dark hole, never to be seen again, and it rarely felt like it was used to your benefit.

My earliest memories centre around my mother cooking – the smell that wafted through our bedrooms on early mornings when she was making bacon and pancakes, playing on the floor of the kitchen with pots and wooden spoons while she spent hours canning jelly, baking holiday treats. Baking and cooking were like breathing to my mother – it was not fancy, it was basic mid-western fare that always tasted amazing. When my brother and I started school and my mother was looking to go back to work, like many women she found her options limited because she still needed to be home in the mornings and afternoons when we were not at school. She turned to her cooking skills and found an open cook and cashier position at our elementary school cafeteria and for the next 25 years my mum became the lunch lady.

She loved her job, her work schedule matched our school schedules, she found a great team to work with and she thoroughly enjoyed working with children every day – sharing smiles and stories and a dose of motherly care as they passed her in the lunch line year after year. In all her years as the beloved lunch lady in her school, I only heard her complain once. About five years into her chosen career, the position of head baker came open at her school and like I said, my mother was a natural at all things baking and cooking. For the last few years she had been the primary substitute for the baker when she was on leave and it was a known fact that my mother's peanut-butter squares rivalled those of every cook in the district. Everyone assumed she would get the job, but there was a hitch.

Years earlier someone in the district HR function decided that the head baker at every school was required to take a series of tests and assessments for this specific job. The tests consisted of maths and word problems that would rival any high school equivalency test and for my amazing mother they were a real barrier. Although my mother had never been diagnosed, it was pretty clear she had mild dyslexia that she had lived with all her life, a learning difference that involves the way the brain processes graphic symbols and impairs a person's ability to read and write. For my mother it meant written test taking was excruciating. The sad thing was that there was no connection between bakers who passed this test and better baking skills or the ability to actually do the job. It had been an arbitrary decision made by someone who understood that converting measurements was an important skill but created a test that measured reading and writing more than the actual skill needed for the job. It took my mum two years of hard work and the support of her entire kitchen staff, but she finally passed that test – and became head baker for her school for another 20 years.

The sad part is that all the effort that went into that test did not make her a better baker. The data from her first five attempts at the test was not used to create a learning plan to help my mother, and the test data was not used to improve the job in any way or even improve the process for hiring for that position. She received no feedback on any of the assessments or tests she took for that role, and no one really assessed her ability to actually bake throughout the entire process. It was literally an exercise in ticking the box, positioned as a compliance requirement but not really required by anyone but the district's HR function. All the energy my mother put into that test was a loss to the school and our family, and almost caused her to walk away from a job she really wanted. Every time an organization asks an employee to take a test or an assessment, provide data or otherwise share information with an organization, it should have a clear plan of how that information will be used, and more importantly how that use will benefit the organization and the employee.

Human Resources has a long tradition of collecting immense amounts of data that go unused and that perception has only intensified as HR increases the use of multiple HR systems. As soon as organizations start to use this data to influence actual work-related questions, they are practising HR analytics. Once an organization begins to build out enterprise processes, functions and metrics to inform business outcomes, it is leveraging HR business intelligence. And when an organization is leveraging both internal workforce data and external data to predict outcomes, conduct scenario planning and inform business strategy, it is practising enterprise workforce planning.

In 2020 only 39 per cent of organizations in Sapient Insights' Annual HR Systems Survey (Figure 9.1) felt they were using their current HR Technology environments to inform their business or organizational strategies, a disappointing outcome for organizations that invested millions in these applications. The adoption of core HR,

FIGURE 9.1   Perception of how HR Technology is being used in organizations, 2020

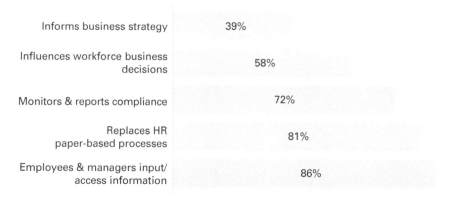

Level of HR Technology utilization

Informs business strategy	39%
Influences workforce business decisions	58%
Monitors & reports compliance	72%
Replaces HR paper-based processes	81%
Employees & managers input/ access information	86%

service delivery, time and talent applications provides an organization with clear benefits in the areas of HR efficiency and process management. However, the real value of these systems is realized in using the data from these applications to help inform employees and managers in better decision making, and ultimately the organization on strategic direction. Unfortunately, in many cases organizations still need to extract the data from their existing HR applications and place it into other applications specifically designed to analyze and visualize data to achieve those final outcomes.

Applications and tools that support workforce analytics and planning efforts help organizations to capture, store, govern, analyze, report and share past and present views of workforce data. The applications may also provide statistical analysis and proprietary algorithms that can deliver insights, recommendations, predictions and forecasts to be used for decision-making purposes. These applications can be focused solely on workforce analytics and planning efforts or share space with other enterprise applications, providing the opportunity to cross-analyze data from all areas of the organization as well as from external sources.

The definitions

Before looking at the types of applications that meet the needs of this HR systems category as seen in Figure 9.2, it is helpful to understand the various types of analytics and planning that are generally required when running an organization and how they might be used when making workforce decisions.

Analytics

The simple definition of analytics is the science of analyzing raw data in order to identify patterns or conclusions from the data. There are generally four types of analytics that are run on organizational data:

- **Descriptive analytics** – describing or summarizing existing data, generally using basic analysis tools or existing application reporting

FIGURE 9.2   Analytics and planning applications category

or dashboards to better understand what happened in the past or is happening currently. The most common analysis techniques in descriptive statistics include basic mathematics, such as sums, mean, median, max, percentage, on existing data.

- o An organization may run a descriptive analysis of its employee demographics to identify the percentage of female versus male applicants that were hired in the last 12 months.

- **Diagnostic analytics** – analyzing past performance to determine 'what' happened and 'why' it happened, sometimes using more advanced analysis tools outside of existing applications to look for patterns, impact factors and unseen connections. The most common analysis techniques in diagnostic analytics include drill-down efforts, data discovery, data mining and correlations.

- o An organization may run a diagnostic analysis to drill down on specific regions or teams that hire more females and assess whether its hiring practices are different from those of its counterparts that hire fewer females.

- **Predictive analytics** – using past data and additional inputs to predict possible future outcomes, almost always requiring a separate application or module outside of existing applications. The common analysis techniques are advanced statistical modelling and machine learning that may create forecasts, classification of expected individual behaviours, time-related cycles or analysis of clusters with expected behaviours.

- o An organization runs a predictive analysis that estimates the percentage of female employees who are likely to work for the organization in three years if the current processes in hiring, onboarding and development remain unchanged.

- **Prescriptive analytics** – a type of predictive analytics that recommends multiple courses of action based on the analyzed data; the focus is on finding the best course of action. Prescriptive analytics uses data from all the other analytics methods and applies additional models to assess the impact and value of possible decisions.

○ A prescriptive analytics model recommended several options for changes that could be made to hiring, onboarding and development processes to improve the likelihood that the organization would achieve a higher percentage of women in key leadership roles in three years. Each recommendation had varying degrees of effort, expense, likelihood of success and adverse impacts that also needed to be assessed.

Organizational/business planning

This is the process of setting an organization's goals, strategy and future actions with the purpose of increasing its ability to grow, increase financial outcomes, meet its mission or increase future sustainability. Organizational/business planning is always an analysis of investment and risk in relation to the possibility of positive outcomes.

A planning process generally takes these steps:

- Identify the problems, opportunities or outcomes you are trying to achieve.
- Inventory and forecast the market (environmental) conditions.
- Formulate multiple approaches to addressing the needs or achieving the outcomes.
- Evaluate the risks and benefits of various approaches.
- Select the best plan or plans and set milestones and measurements of success.
- Continuously evaluate the progress made towards the plan and adjust as needed.

There are also multiple levels of planning that are conducted inside organizations, including strategic (long-term vision), operational (methods for reaching the strategic plan), tactical (activities and time-lines for reaching the plan) and contingency (alternative courses of action addressing known and unknown risks) planning.

Planning in the Human Resources function generally focuses on the people side of organizational planning. The most common types of HR planning include:

- **Labour forecasting or budgeting** – we discussed this in the time management section of the book, but there is a planning step where organizations assess the total number of staffing/worked hours an organization will require in the future based on business plans or market knowledge. The planning starts with past worked hours and assesses future worked hours, based on existing headcount, and the information is then used to assess the need to increase existing employee hours or to hire more employees. This data is then used to inform headcount planning and strategic workforce planning efforts.

  - We are expecting our customer service calls to double next year and based on the current number of hours worked to meet this year's demand for customer service calls, we will need to require the existing team to work overtime 30 per cent of the time next year or hire five new employees to work the additional hours.

- **Headcount planning** – this is the most basic form of HR planning, focusing on specific job roles or positions and the number of headcount (employees) needed in those job roles to achieve an organization's business plan. Basic headcount planning is generally driven by a financial goal and is often used to figure out a basic number or budget for hiring or for retention plans in the future. These plans may also include workforce location costs (space).

  - This year our revenue was $2.1 million and we had five customer services positions to meet that need. Next year we plan to double our revenue to $5 million, so our new headcount plan needs to increase by 5 customer service positions or a total of 10 customer service employees.

- **Organizational design** – this is a process for assessing, changing, modifying and developing an organization's structure, including leadership roles, reporting relationships, shift patterns, span of control, service delivery models, team configurations and job role design, to optimally achieve your organizational plans. This planning usually requires organizational charting tools and scenario-planning capabilities.

o We currently have five business units, with an average of 500 employees in each unit. There is a separate HR function for each business unit. Each unit handles recruiting, hiring and training very differently. After conducting a thorough organizational design assessment and planning effort, we have identified the opportunity to implement a shared service function that would centralize HR services and standardize many processes for all five business units, but also recommend creating an HR business partner role with dual responsibilities to the business unit and shared services HR function.

- **Targeted workforce planning** – this is a joint planning process between HR and operations for proactively analyzing, forecasting and planning workforce supply and demand for a specific function, role or business unit based on strategic organization planning. This process is more than a headcount or labour analysis as it continuously assesses position/skills gaps, conducts internal and external market analysis, and determines targeted talent and time management interventions aligned with desired business outcomes. Targeted workforce planning is often used for critical skill areas, high turnover functions, high-growth categories, or in preparation for change or contingency events. It usually creates a multi-year solution that has clearly defined milestones and success measurements.

  o In the next two years the organization's strategic plan included rolling out a new category of products that would require a highly engaged call centre support team. Call centres for the current products were already experiencing high turnover and low employee engagement. A targeted workforce planning effort assessed the current organizational structures, the labour schedules and the headcount plans, as well as skillsets, engagement concerns and the available candidate pool in the various hiring markets, and compared these to the desired long-term outcomes. The planning efforts outlined a strategy for addressing cultural issues that were impacting turnover rates, adjusting salary ranges for specific technical call centre roles, a local hiring plan that focused on competencies over previous experience, increasing diversity throughout the entire call centre talent pool, and incentives for an internal development programme that would prepare at least 50 per cent of existing call centre employees for the new role.

- **Enterprise or strategic workforce planning** – this is a joint effort between HR, operations and finance for proactively analyzing, forecasting and planning workforce supply and demand throughout the organization, based on long-term strategic plans and over a period of time. This process uses data and insights gathered from all other HR planning efforts and conducts internal and external market analysis that focuses on the demographics, skills, competencies, roles, salaries and positions required to achieve the desired enterprise strategy. This planning also looks at cultural factors such as organizational structures, leadership and engagement levels as well as environmental factors such as tools, technology and location data. The planning may also assess other work models that include automation, outsourcing, temporary workforces or acquisitions. Enterprise workforce planning requires the ability to run multiple scenarios and simulations, as well as analyze for risk factors, gaps from current state and most important performance indicators. This planning looks across various functions and business units and assesses skills, capabilities and needs at an enterprise level.

    ○ The high-tech organization had a strategic goal to acquire 15 per cent of the market share for its application within two years, while increasing revenues by 10 per cent and maintaining operating costs. To accomplish this goal, it identified three strategic imperatives that it assessed would increase the organization's sales and market share, including a new key product feature, new customer care function and improved sales process. HR, operations and finance worked together on an enterprise workforce planning strategy. They ran several enterprise-level workforce planning scenarios and finally decided on a plan that focused on increasing diversity in their engineering staff, which would improve the organization's product outcomes, hiring key positions in the sales division with capabilities to build out the new sales process and creating an internal mobility programme that would provide a path for existing highly skilled team members to move into the new customer care organization. They identified the HR and operational metrics that would be used to continuously monitor the strategy in relation to the business goals and developed several contingency plans in case any of the performance indicators failed to reach the expected levels at certain milestones.

The category of HR analytics and planning applications is still in its infancy and organizations use a wide range of applications to actually accomplish basic reporting, analysis and planning in HR.

Organizations that are extremely serious about being data-driven, those that have hired data scientists and have large HR analytics functions, are likely to also have exceptionally large employee data sets. These organizations use a mixture of programming tools to develop custom algorithms and machine learning models, along with data storage tools, standard analytics tools and planning solutions to create custom HR reporting and forecasting for their leaders.

- **Algorithm** – a process or set of rules to be followed in calculations or problem-solving operations, usually by a computer.
- **Machine learning** – the use and development of computer systems that are able to learn and adapt without following explicit instructions by using algorithms and statistical models to analyze and draw inference from patterns.

Today, most organizations with an average employee size can leverage off-the-shelf solutions for their HR analytics and planning needs. These applications currently exist as a combination of enterprise platform technologies, embedded analytics solutions inside existing HR or business applications, or as stand-alone multi-use data cleansing, analytics or visualization tools. We also see a growing number of dedicated HR-specific analytics and planning suites. Some organizations analyze data directly in the various HR systems, while others extract data into data warehouses or data lakes and run their analysis from these environments.

Although many of these applications have overlapping features and capabilities, here is a general breakdown of the most common application types and examples in this category:

- **Embedded HR analytics** – separate modules within an organization's core HRMS, service delivery, time management and talent management platforms that can be turned on or installed but are not sold separately from the application. Capabilities can vary widely by solution but can include various levels of descriptive and basic diagnostic capabilities, as well as predefined predictive and prescriptive analytics. These applications often include dashboards, interactive reports and data communication tools.

o Examples of these types of applications include UKG Pro HR Workforce Intelligence, Cornerstone Reporting and Analytics, Workforce Software Analytics and Insights, TalentSoft Analytics, SAP SuccessFactors Workforce Analytics, Qualtrics Employee XM.

- **Data management and manipulation** – tools designed to extract large amounts of data for storage, organization and mapping that is then made available to individuals to run processes or algorithms. These are generally called data warehouses for structured data and data lakes for unstructured data. These applications are generally the domain of the IT function, but it is important for the analytics team to be part of the configuration decisions, data pulling schedules and data mapping efforts.

o Examples of these types of tools include Amazon Redshift, Oracle Autonomous Data Warehouse, Informatica Power, Teradata.

- **Extraction and analysis** – tools used to extract specific data from various systems and to conduct cleansing, organizing and categorization, and to run separate unique analysis.

o Examples of these types of tools include SQL, R, Python as well as applications like Microsoft Excel, SaS Viya, Alteryx, IBM SPSS Statistics, Qlik Analytics Platform, Tableau Prep, Oracle Business Intelligence, MicroStrategy.

- **Visualization and sharing** – tools generally designed to use clean data, defined data and large data sets to produce images, charts, communications and presentations. These applications often allow an organization to embed linked charts or images into other applications, allowing for regularly updated data as well as the capability to drill into the embedded data.

o Examples of these types of tools include Microsoft Power BI, Tableau Online, QlikView/Sense.

- **HR analytics and planning platforms** – applications that can be purchased separately from any specific HR application. They are platforms built specifically for HR queries. They generally have the ability to integrate multiple HR data sets, along with non-HR data sets including operations data, industry benchmarking data, regional government data and other factors that might be needed to contextualize or inform an analysis of HR data. Due to the industry focus, these applications often have pre-built tools for data integration, cleaning and categorization. They can run custom analysis, but often include pre-set analysis for benchmarking, forecasting and prediction efforts to help provide more insights. These applications vary greatly in their feature sets.

  ◦ Examples of these types of tools include Visier, HiQLabs, OrgVue, OneModel.

- **Business intelligence and analytics platforms** – these applications may be stand-alone or part of existing enterprise business platforms such as Oracle or SAP. They are generally designed as platforms built for financial reporting and business queries. They have the ability to integrate multiple data sets, including internal and external data that might be needed to contextualize or inform a business decision. These applications generally have pre-built integrations and data cleaning and categorization tools. They are designed to run custom analysis and forecast planning, and to produce reports and dashboards necessary for business operations. Older versions of these applications are very structured in the type of data they can analyze and the need for an IT resource to adjust queries, while newer applications are leveraging advanced machine learning to analyze unstructured data as well as natural language processing to enable a more user-friendly environment. These applications vary greatly in their feature sets.

  ◦ Examples of these types of tools include, Workday Prism Analytics, Oracle Analytics Cloud, SAP Analytics Cloud, SAP Business Objects, IBM Cognos Analytics, Tableau, ThoughtSpot, Sisense.

- **Business planning and forecasting applications** – applications designed specifically to manage extra large amounts of historical data, categorize it for planning purposes, and run multiple forecasting scenarios and business models. These are often designed specifically for financial analysis and reporting, but newer applications are expanding into broader planning that includes HR, operations and other categories. The application may also be able to create planning dashboards and provide diagnostic drill-down capabilities.
  - Examples of these types of tools include Anaplan, Workday Adaptive Planning, Oracle Hyperion, Oracle EPM Cloud, SAP Analytics Cloud.

Generally, organizations are using a mixture of these applications to manage their HR analytics and planning processes, just as they do for HR administrative, talent and time management processes. On average, organization are using 3.7 different solutions, including their embedded HR Tools, to create, store, govern, analyze, report and share past, present and future workforce information.[1] The most popular tool in this category continues to be Microsoft Excel, with 93 per cent of organizations identifying it as a tool used during their analytics and planning process (Figure 9.3).

FIGURE 9.3   Analytics and planning application adoption, 2020

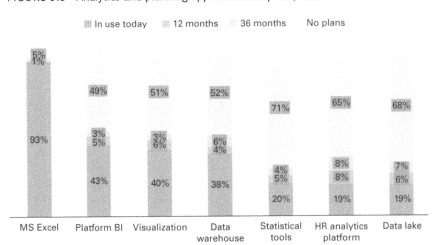

One of the big challenges in this category is the large number of times that data is often downloaded to personal computers or desktop applications to be transformed in some way and then re-uploaded to other applications. Like any other workflow and data management process, the data included in these critical analysis efforts often includes sensitive organizational information, employee data or personal identifiable information. Handling this type of data carefully is not just good business, it is often required by law.

- **Personal identifiable information** – any data that could potentially be used to identify a person's identity either alone or when combined with other personal or identifying information that is linked or linkable to specific individual data. Examples include a full name, social security number, driving licence number, bank account number, passport number and email address.

There are multiple regional regulations and compliance standards concerning how organizations must protect and handle personal identifiable information, and reporting requirements if the data is breached.

Additionally, any analysis that is being run on a regular basis or any algorithm that is used to provide predictive or prescriptive data must be clearly defined and easily explainable before an organization should feel comfortable using that data to make decisions that may impact the organization, employees or customers. These applications, data analysis tools and data sets also require constant calibration, alignment and management to ensure that the analysis is using the right data, the data is clean enough for a full analysis, the sample size is large enough, and known biases in the data sets are addressed or minimized by additional modelling efforts.

The history of HR reporting and workforce planning

In the United States following the stock market crash of 1929 and the Great Depression, the US government granted the Securities and Exchange Commission (SEC) the authority to set standards for accounting practices to reduce the likelihood of future stock market crashes. The SEC delegated this responsibility to the American Institute of Accountants, which eventually gave way to the Financial Accounting Standards Board (FASB) and the creation in 1973 of the Generally Accepted Accounting Principles (GAAP).[2]

GAAP sets objectives and guidelines for financial statements and reporting calculations. There are three major sets of rules covered in GAAP: basic accounting principles and guidelines, detailed standards of the FASB and generally accepted industry practices.[3] Within the guidelines set by GAAP, auditors attempt to establish uniformity among the financial reports of publicly traded companies. Many non-public companies follow them as well. These standards provide a way for organizations to understand the financial health of an organization more easily before planning to lend money, invest, purchase or work with an organization. Similar accounting standards are followed in 140 countries around the world governed by the International Financial Reporting Standards (IFRS) overseen by the International Accounting Standards Board (IASB).[4]

The important thing to note is that for almost 100 years countries have been focusing on standardizing financial reporting and metrics, and since 1973 most organizations have had some general guidelines for the metrics, reporting and planning needed in financial functions to assess the health of an organization. There are GAAP requirements concerning the reporting of compensation, stock-based compensation, employee retirement funds and total number of employees, but in general the Human Resources function does not have similar standards or guidelines set for those purposes. There are plenty of compliance and reporting requirements for various government entities that focus on employee health and safety, hiring practices or firing practices, but this data is not generally included in an organization's public documentation for the assessment of the organization's viability.

This lack of standards has left organizations to come up with an individual perspective on what should be monitored and assessed in organizations for the wellbeing of their Human Resources practices. It also means that even if two organizations use similar language to describe the value or health of their HR practices such as high engagement, low turnover or skills readiness, these terms can have quite different meanings in different companies.

EXAMPLES

The average turnover in one retail organization is over 100 per cent of employees annually, so low turnover in that environment would be considered 80 per cent. Voluntary and involuntary turnover rates are reported as a single metric.

The average turnover in an electric co-op is extremely low annually, so low turnover is 5 per cent. The organization actually has a challenge giving new employees an opportunity to move up in the organization, so it only reports voluntary turnover in the 3–5-year employment range as a critical issue.

We are seeing some slight movement in the space of standard human capital management reporting in the last few years. In 2020, the SEC made a new rule that mandates, for the first time, public reporting of human capital metrics by companies subject to SEC reporting requirements. The new rule requires the number of employees to be reported and encourages companies to report the number of full-time, part-time and temporary employees as well as independent contractors and contingent workers if they are material to an understanding of the company's business. 'Material' is anything an investor should know before buying or selling a stock, bond or derivative.

The new rule also mandates, for the first time, that companies provide 'to the extent such disclosure is material to an understanding of the registrant's business taken as a whole, a description of a registrant's human capital resources, including any human capital measures or objectives that the registrant focuses on in managing the business'. The SEC continues to specifically call out the three areas of 'attraction, development and retention of personnel as non-exclusive examples of subjects that may be material, depending on the registrant's business and workforce'.[5]

These SEC standards were actually derived from the International Organization for Standardization (ISO) Human Capital Reporting Standards, which call for a much broader set of standards, including 10 specific metrics for public reporting by all organizations, 13 additional metrics for reporting by larger organizations and 36 other metrics for internal reporting.[6]

The major areas covered in the ISO reporting standards include:

- ethics;
- costs (total workforce);
- workforce diversity;
- leadership (trust);
- organizational safety, health and wellbeing;
- productivity (EBIT/revenue/turnover/profit per employee, etc);
- recruitment, mobility and turnover;
- skills and capabilities (total development and training costs);
- workforce availability (number of employees, full-time equivalents).

These standards will take years to become clearly defined and comparable across organizations, but they are a step in the necessary direction of valuing an organization's Human Resources practices as highly as it values its financial practices.

Reporting standards are just the tip of the iceberg when it comes to the historical challenges with analytics and planning in the Human Resources industry. There are also challenges with our available analysis tools and data sets. Although we have been studying human behaviour for hundreds of years, our analysis tools for predicting future behaviour have been relatively unaltered and often make broad generalizations based on expected decisions or past behaviours.

For example, traditional economic models assumed for years both that people would always be rational in their financial decision making, assuming that an individual may make a poor financial decision, and that the larger community would always balance out the data and predictions by making rational financial decisions. Recent discoveries in human psychology and practical understanding of incentives and market behaviour have shown that a new approach to predicting outcomes through behavioural economics can provide much better indicators of long-term outcomes and decision making.[7]

Similarly, organizations that rely on machine learning and predictive analytics are plagued with historically biased training data (data used to train machine learning engines) that is less likely to include people of colour, women or neurodiverse employees. This type of bias not only creates false positives when looking for critical skills and characteristics for successful employee outcomes, it also incorrectly places lower values on other characteristics that are more likely to achieve long-term outcomes.

For example, a hiring assessment looks at the past five years of top-performing sales executives to identify the skills, competencies and behaviours aligned with success in that career. The data clearly identifies an extroverted personality that is highly competitive, with strong communication and interpersonal skills. If you did further diagnostic analysis you would also find that a high percentage of top-performing sales executives graduated from three specific universities. Without further analysis and some context setting to the data, it might have been missed that the vice-president in each group graduated from one of these three universities. Upon further inspection it is identified that these top sales executives were given existing sales relationships and more support from senior leadership in building new relationships. Sales executives who received new territories and less relationship support were more likely to be from diverse backgrounds, women, black or Latino team members. The data is clearly biased in multiple ways and should not be used for analysis.

Why you need to care

People costs often account for nearly 70–80 per cent of all operating costs of an organization, and for many, people are the major creator of value, but historically analysis of the workforce has either been missed or has been done purely from a headcount and cost perspective. Once purely the domain of large organizations with enough resources and data to make HR analytics and planning a valuable effort, today even the smallest organization is finding beneficial outcomes from understanding its workforce through a data lens.

Even with the current challenges that exist in technology and data management efforts, the future of HR is in data. No matter your HR position, you will be expected to understand and be able to work with the various data sets that are part of the HR Technology environment. You will be expected to understand the value in tracking various HR metrics, how often they should be reviewed and the context that is needed to understand the data.

Organizations will increasingly see more and more embedded HR analysis tools as part of their HR systems, and although technology is providing significant opportunities to conduct ongoing analysis of workforce data that was previously uneconomical, technology should not drive the decision on what HR questions are being answered by the analysis process. Many organizations fall into the trap of analyzing what is easy to analyze, not what has the highest potential value to the organization. For example, over 50 per cent of organizations are using their HR analytics tools to manage HR costs and address risk management through compliance tracking, but just over 30 per cent of organizations are using these tools to ensure they are assigning optimal work assignments or have the skills needed for critical workforce plans.[8]

Those organizations that take the time to invest in a culture of data-driven HR decision making benefit from having a complete picture of their past, present and future possibilities as an organization. Research has shown that data-driven HR functions continuously see significantly higher HR, talent and business outcomes over their non-data-driven peers – over a five-year period, data-driven HR functions saw an average of 11 per cent higher outcomes year over year, an even better percentage of improved outcomes than simply being focused on talent or financial decision making.[9] These organizations were also more likely to conduct enterprise or strategic workforce planning, another characteristic that has aligned with better business outcomes for multiple years.

This is the time to rethink our role in HR and to consider what it means to be strategic in both our approach to HR and our supporting systems. As we noted earlier, just 39 per cent of organizations said their HR system environments were being utilized to inform business strategy, and tightly connected to this measure is the fact that 36 per cent of organizations stated they were practising enterprise work-force planning; in 2020 this was a 30 per cent increase over the previous year, as many organizations expanded workforce planning efforts in response to the economic downturn and health crisis. When it was absolutely necessary, HR functions figured out how to get the data and leverage their tools to provide the answers for their leaders and employees, supporting large enterprise pivots, work-from-home mandates and redeployment of skilled workers. We saw amazing stories of courage, community and innovation in 2020 that provide a model for what the future of HR could look like if we leverage the tools and data we have in our organizations.

HANDS-ON ACTIVITIES

- Who owns workforce planning in your organization? If no one, why do you think this is not a priority?
- Identify whether your organization has an HR analytics role, function or department.
  - If yes, interview at least two members of the team and learn about their job roles.
  - If no, identify what roles in the organization are responsible for HR reporting and interview those people.
- Identify whether HR has regular reporting or dashboards that are shared with senior leaders/executives.
- If yes, ask if any of these metrics or data sets are included in the regular reporting:
  - employee demographics (age, gender, race)
  - employee voluntary or involuntary turnover
  - time to hire or open recruiting requisitions
  - compensation bands or pay equity analysis
  - absence or leave data

- o performance management or operations performance data
- o development plans or completed training
- o workforce productivity
- Identify whether any of these applications are in use currently and whether they are part of a suite of technologies, a point solution or not in use at all.

TABLE 9.1

HR analytics and planning applications	Application use and deployment model				
	Not in use	ERP suite	HR suite	Analytics suite	Point solution
HR analytics module (embedded)					
Data analytics tool					
Data visualization tool					
Data warehouse or data lake					
HR analytics and planning platforms					
Business intelligence and analytics platform					
Business planning and forecasting tool					

- Identify who in your organization has access to HR analytics tools or dashboards:

  - o HR staff
  - o IT/HRIT

- o executives
- o managers
- o finance staff
- o shared services
- o all employees
- Identify whether your organization conducts any of these types of workforce planning efforts:
  - o Labour forecasting or budgeting
  - o Headcount planning
  - o Targeted workforce planning
  - o Enterprise or strategic workforce planning
- If yes, identify who owns the process and interview them on the process steps, data included in the process and the tools used to complete the process.

CASE STUDY
The human side of analytics and planning

When organizations grow quickly, accurate planning is imperative. If demand outpaces organizational resources, customer satisfaction may be irreparably damaged before operations can be scaled to meet current needs, and critical employees can face burnout.

A consulting firm founded in the early 2000s quickly grew from a start-up to a medium-sized company expanding services internationally. The rapid increase in demand and growth placed a huge demand on existing disconnected finance and human resource solutions. The team needed a more accurate and informative view of project and resource management, time and expense tracking, and analytics. They also faced challenges in financial and workforce planning, which was a manual process using spreadsheets. Reporting took extra time and resources to gather data from all the different systems. There were regular questions about data quality, which trickled down to budgeting and planning and forecasting, often leading to delayed decision making.

The organization decided that a single system covering financial management, workforce planning, HR and professional services automation would be best for them, ultimately choosing a cloud ERP solution with both Finance and HR applications.

With a single platform, HR professionals now had workforce planning and talent management working together in one system, giving them complete visibility into their workforce. Putting people at the core of the company allowed them to recruit top candidates, and nurture and train employees with critical skill sets. Senior management could make decisions faster and more accurately with a single view of organizational data. The firm can now see the precise amount of margin on every project and make business decisions accordingly; for example if the margin drops below a certain threshold, the project manager is informed and can tell employees when taking appropriate action. Employees benefit from an intuitive user experience using through their preferred devices, which gives them a greater degree of autonomy, while managers feel more empowered.

Planning is not something that just happens once a year, or at an enterprise level, and as we noted earlier, the various levels of planning require engagement, trusted data and visibility into possible outcomes based on the decisions made by executives, frontline leaders and employees. .

Endnotes

1   Sapient Insights, 2020–2021 HR Systems Survey White Paper, 23rd Annual Edition

2   FASB (nd) About the FASB, www.fasb.org/facts/ (archived at https://perma.cc/ M5GJ-SJZ8)

3   FASB (nd) About the FASB, www.fasb.org/facts/ (archived at https://perma.cc/ M5GJ-SJZ8)

4   FASB (nd) Comparability in international accounting standards – a brief history, www.fasb.org/jsp/FASB/Page/SectionPage&cid=1176156304264 (archived at https://perma.cc/G4W8-LYL4)

5   Vance, D (2020) The SEC has published its final rule on human capital reporting *Chief Learning Officer* www.chieflearningofficer.com/2020/09/03/ the-sec-has-published-its-final-rule-on-human-capital-reporting/ (archived at https://perma.cc/KQ4U-53T3)

6   Naden, C (2019) New ISO international standard for human capital reporting, *ISO* www.iso.org/news/ref2357.html (archived at https://perma.cc/9DFW-V6VS); see also: ISO 30414:2018(en) Human resource management – guidelines for internal and external human capital reporting, www.iso.org/obp/ ui/#iso:std:iso:30414:ed-1:v1:en (archived at https://perma.cc/MSV6-UGDE)

7   Thaler, R, (2015) *Misbehaving: The making of behavioral economics*, Allen Lane

8   Sapient Insights, 2020–2021 HR Systems Survey White Paper, Series HR Analytics and Planning Bytes

9   Sapient Insights (Sierra-Cedar) 2019–2020 HR Systems Survey White Paper, 22nd Annual Edition

10

Emerging HR Technology and the future of work

Introduction

In 1982 my father got a part-time job for the sole purpose of making enough extra money to buy a personal computer. Everyone around him had an opinion about investing extra time and money into something so unusual. Most thought he was crazy – why not spend the extra money on a family vacation or a new car? Others thought he was on the cutting edge of a world that was really out of reach for anyone in our little blue-collar town.

My dad had a vision, though. In his vision the world looked a lot more like his favourite TV show, *Star Trek*, and a lot less like the manual hard-working world he lived in. He wanted to be an educator and he believed the future of education was in the computer. Within a year he had saved enough money to make the purchase, a shiny new Apple IIe, with a colour monitor, a floppy disk drive and a keyboard that could input both lower-case and capital letters. We were the first ones on the block to have anything like it, and visitors would stand around our dining room table marvelling at games like 'Oregon Trail' and 'Cranston Manor' while all the kids fought to type the commands.

My mother, who everyone knew had to approve the purchase, was not quite as taken with this new-fangled interloper to her dining room table. She knew it was important to my dad's future, but she wasn't exactly sure how, and it wasn't helping her in any way with the things she needed help with every day: managing the house, meals, yardwork. There were other issues too – it was too big to fit on the small family desk she used for bills, so for months it was a permanent fixture on her dining room table. The initial expense was not the final investment needed to get the most out of our exorbitant purchase: it required software, a new desk and chair, and the expense of adding a plug to the wall. Her biggest frustration though, by far, was that it occupied her primary household workers non-stop. My younger brother and I, usually her constant companions to help with yard and housework, were glued to this device and she had to employ various levels of threats, incentives and, the worst of all, raising her usually calm voice to the level that quickly told us we had gone too far to get us away from its glowing screen.

Working with emerging technology inside organizations is not much different from the experience my family faced with our new computer. Every organization has to weigh the expense, risks and benefits of investing in technology before it has been proven to achieve the outcomes it promises. Our existing environments are often poorly designed to use new technologies or to take advantage of their benefits without additional investments in hardware, software, employee education or process changes. Organizations often invest large amounts upfront in researching and developing emerging technologies only to find they have unintended outcomes that may impact employees or customers adversely and outweigh the initial benefits. The payoff for upfront investments may come years down the road or actually be achieved by other organizations that learned from your initial risks and possible failures. It all seems so risky, why take the leap? Well, the rewards can be just as big. Catching the next wave in emerging technology before anyone else can propel your company ahead of the competition and give your employees just enough advantage to create amazing outcomes.

Our family's early investment did not pay off right away, it took my father another five years before he could translate that investment into a classroom full of computers and change a basic vocational electrician high school programme into an award-winning curriculum for a state-of-the-art electronics programme, teaching the earliest forms of programmable logic controllers (PLCs). My mother eventually forgave us for our earlier obsessions and beamed with pride when computers were introduced into our junior high classes, and teachers were amazed with the knowledge we brought to the classroom. Unfortunately, neither my brother nor I was born to be a programmer and my dad's hopes that we would make our fortunes in the computer industry dwindled quickly – but because of those early successes I always gravitated towards using technology in my career in ways that improved outcomes. Emerging technology rarely ends up achieving exactly what we thought it would when it was first envisioned – who knew the phone would become our personal assistant, or HR administrative software focused on efficiency would actually end up being the greatest data source in an organization? Often the greatest value in emerging technology is that it requires you to look at the world a little differently.

The definitions

Innovation in the business world comes in many formats, the least of which is simply new and bigger technology. The next generation of business technology is being designed to inform our decisions and simplify our activities; it is meant to be invisible and ubiquitous in our lives and expected to perform as an intelligent system. All emerging technologies have a place in history, but not all of them will have enterprise-wide impact or be of value to an organization over time.

A general definition of emerging technology is technology that is currently in development or expected to be available to the public/ businesses within the next 5–10 years. The term is usually reserved for technology that is expected to create a significant impact on businesses, employees or clients in the future. There is always a revolving door of emerging technology experiments being developed into the coolest next thing, along with those once-novel ideas that are rapidly losing steam as they prove to add less value than expected.

Another important factor in this topic is understanding that innovation is not the same thing as emerging technology. Organizations can be very innovative and never invest in emerging technology, and they can invest heavily in emerging technology and never actually be innovative.

FIGURE 10.1 Emerging technology

VALUING THE CHAOS OF INNOVATION

In an era of intelligent systems, self-driving cars and personal tracking devices, the topic of innovation is permanently tied to major technological advances. The idea of bigger, faster and more advanced computer technology seems like the ultimate goal, with innovation driving us ever onwards. In reality, the greatest innovations yet to be achieved are distinctly lacking in technological focus – particularly in the arena of Human Resources. HR Technology may provide a support mechanism for many of these innovations, but the areas of real ingenuity are more likely to come from organizational design, health and wellness, or community mobilization models. Research areas such as neuroscience, psychology and behavioural decision making may become more critical to tomorrow's HR innovations than specific technical skills are today. If those research areas make you a bit uncomfortable and nervous, that is ok because real life-changing innovations are generally outside the comfort level of everyday organizations.

The allure of innovation feels endless. It is placed upon a pedestal like a shining beacon of hope. Our books and movies are filled with tenacious innovation heroes: Jobs, the Wright Brothers, Edison, Da Vinci, Marie Curie – each honoured for their pioneering spirit and life-changing innovations. When the idea of innovation is viewed only through the rose-coloured lenses of success, it is easy to see why so many organizations aspire to be seen as innovative. In reality, innovation is messy, painful and beleaguered by years of failure.

Early innovators are often lost to time. They have names like Siegfried Marcus, a little-known inventor from Vienna who created a 'mobile internal combustion engine' – the world's first automobile.[1] Those first 'out-of-the-box thinkers' are often mocked for their initial efforts, scorned for their lack of traditional values, even shunned for the heresy of their new beliefs, and often lack the funding required to support their work. Behind each great name connected with a major innovation that was finally mainstreamed and accepted you will find a line of less accepted innovators paving the way before them.

Real innovation creates chaos and turmoil; it challenges traditional work and hierarchies; it raises questions, it is inefficient and costly. When most organizations aspire to build a culture of innovation, it is rare that they understand what this truly entails. A culture of innovation, or more aptly put an environment where innovation thrives, is one that understands and embraces the chaos of innovation and values the process as much as the outcome.

Although innovation seems like a lofty goal, it is fair to say that not every organization needs to chase the life-changing innovation environment required to achieve major new outcomes. Generally, systems and organizations run more efficiently when they manage their business through incremental change and transparent cultural expectations. Incremental change may not be as popular as the exciting fires of innovation, but it is a more viable short-term business model. Watching the trends carefully, and taking advantage of market changes through acquisition, divestitures, focus and staff augmentation, can create a profitable business for an exceedingly long time. If an organization feels that it is a necessary sustainability goal to become highly innovative, it needs to clearly set expectations for the environment it is building. These are organizations that mix diverse thinkers with different cultural and experiential backgrounds and are prepared for internal conflicts to arise. They give independent and collaborative thinkers equal space and time. They celebrate failure as much as successes, and quickly model and iterate concepts and ideas. They encourage experimentation but provide structure for quick decision making and idea mainstreaming. If they have the resources, they fund innovation and its multiple failures as deeply as they fund their key business areas. If they have a lack of resources, they empower employees with the freedom to rethink the work and how to accomplish the goals, creating environments where necessity is truly the mother of invention. Most importantly, they manage the risk realities of innovations versus fearing the lack of outcomes.

If developing an environment that embraces innovation seems a step too far, some organizations choose to create separate stand-alone functions or even fund separate companies that become the innovation incubators. Given autonomy but still included in the critical feedback process of a transparent organization, these innovation arms can be valuable – as long as they do not work in a bubble or limit the pollination of ideas. These types of organizations can provide opportunities to cycle talented employees from primary businesses to innovation environments and reduce the risk of losing developing talent due to burnout or lack of advancement opportunities. They often provide reduced risk but are not completely risk free. They might have additional funding beyond the initial corporate investment. In some cases, organizations create corporate venture capital funds where major investments are made in existing innovative startups with the idea that over time viable innovative organizations will succeed and become valuable assets of the investing organizations.

In each of these models, HR has a critical role to play in the enterprise-wide discussions concerning innovation. All of our innovation heroes needed a mechanism for mainstreaming their new ideas and putting them into action. HR can advocate for reality, providing leadership with an honest view of whether or not an organization's environment will nurture innovative ideas. No matter where innovative ideas are coming from, HR can help prepare both management and employees for the coming changes. When HR takes a strategic role in the organization, it is not simply reacting to requests for change but rather facilitating the innovation and preparing for the chaos, risks and hopefully the eventual growth from innovative ideas.

For the purposes of this book, we will define and discuss four major areas of emerging technology that are likely to have tangible outcomes for HR and business organizations. We will look at the areas of:

- monitoring technologies;
- communication technologies;
- workflow and automation tools;
- intelligent platforms.

Monitoring technologies

This category of emerging technology is a means of hardware, software or application that is utilized in conjunction with an electronic device that captures, monitors, records or reports information about the user's activities with or without the user's knowledge.

As we noted earlier, HR is all about capturing information and usually through cumbersome forms or hardware specifically created for capturing that information from the workforce. We will always have some form of that in HR, but emerging technology in this category is focused on non-invasive data-capturing techniques. The non-invasive idea sounds great, but it also has an element of creepiness about it that makes everyone a little uneasy with the topic. Every tool that is used to monitor and capture data is also subject to major ethical and regulatory concerns and should be implemented carefully, with clear guidance on the risks.

HR has a plethora of data capturing tools used with employees that range from the generally accepted to early adoption.

- **Surveys and interview tools** – the most accepted monitoring/data capturing tools with the greatest level of use by HR are surveys and interview assessment tools – everything from exit interviews to pulse surveys (quick, short surveys sent out regularly on critical employee topics) falls into this category. The challenge here is survey fatigue – no one likes to constantly be asked for their experience, thoughts, feelings and perceptions, especially if there is not any immediate action the organization can take on that data. Nevertheless, they are valuable tools and pulse surveys are seeing continued growth and innovation.

- **Mobile and wearables** – these are monitoring devices that an employee generally has more control over. Most employees are clearly aware of the programs or devices that are doing the monitoring and can leave these items in a work environment or turn off the tracking devices if they wish, although that may also reduce the ability to clock in to work, have a record of hours and locations worked, access work environments or track the safety, health or engagement of a worker.

- **Video, audio, personal device/desktop monitoring** – these monitoring devices should be discussed in every employee handbook or onboarding programme, but employees often forget about these tools because they are less obvious. The emerging tech side of this industry isn't in the actual capturing of the data – organizations have been using video, audio and desktop monitoring for years, often overseen by audit and loss functions or IT departments monitoring for illegal behaviours. The recent advancements in this area have been focused on computer analysis of these data formats, and algorithms that turn that data into constant feedback on how to optimize work, reduce risks or improve engagement.

- **Biometric or environmental monitoring** – these are monitoring devices that are generally less known about but focus on capturing passive data from the employee, the environment or equipment. The term 'Internet of Things' (IoT) is often used in relation to these monitoring devices as well. These devices are much more extensive than mobile or wearable tracking devices and can capture a wealth of information, but they also cause real concerns over data privacy issues.

  o Biometric monitoring is the tracking of users' characteristics, related to conscious and unconscious changes in human traits and body parameters, such as temperament, motivation, temperature, skin conductance, posture balance, brain activity or heart rate dynamics for assessing users' more complex characteristics like emotions and behaviour. With IoT technology, every biometric monitoring device is able to wirelessly communicate and transmit this data.

  o Environmental monitoring is the process of making sure a particular environment is suitable for its intended purpose. Many industries use environmental monitoring to ensure employees and equipment are safe and able to perform their functions efficiently. Being able to monitor minute changes in an office or worksite makes it less likely that a small action or environmental imbalance will turn into performance deterrents, damaged equipment or safety issues.

Communication technologies

An efficient and effective HR service delivery model includes multiple employee interactions, often across several communication channels. Two-way communications, where information is shared, action is taken and more information is shared back, is the goal of any communication effort. The challenge is that most communication methods are single-directional and organizations have no clue whether the message was received, actions were taken or outcomes were achieved.

In recent years, emerging analysis technology and a wealth of available data from social media outlets have created an abundance of innovation in marketing efforts that help organizations target their messaging, track communication outcomes and even embed human psychology into marketing efforts to influence human behaviour. All of this has been viewed with concern, scepticism and a call for new regulations in the public domain. When scaled down from a less concerning level of 'manipulation' to one of 'personalization', these innovations can be transformational inside an HR function desperately trying to get the right messaging to its candidates and existing workforce. On average, organizations use anywhere from two to three different methods to communicate with their employees and external candidates at any given time, and we are continuing to see that number increase every year as organizations leverage new tools that help them use multiple delivery mechanisms for their messaging.

The emerging technology currently being embedded in the HR Technology and communication systems landscape is likely to change the dynamics of every HR Technology platform in the near future, as it changes the primary way an organization interacts with it audience. Organizations are quickly realizing that they need to reach candidates and employees with the critical messages where they are at, versus pulling them into yet another HR platform or tool.

Emerging technology in the form of communication methods today includes:

- personalized, tailored and actionable emails;
- personalized portals or hubs of information;
- call centres with automated workflow assistants;
- live chat and automated chatbots;
- targeted social media messaging;
- direct mobile and text messaging tools;
- conversational interfaces.

All these new communication methods start and end with data and data analysis and provide HR functions with more insight into what communications are being heard, how those communications are being received and what actions their audiences are taking.

Workflow and automation tools

A workflow is a sequence of tasks that processes a set of data within an organization. Any time that data is passed between humans and/or systems, a workflow is created. Workflow automation refers to the design, execution and automation of processes based on workflow rules where human tasks, data or files are routed between people or systems based on pre-defined business rules. Every HR system is built on some level of workflows, but a major part of most HRMS systems is the ability for administrators to set up their own specific workflows based on the unique needs of the organization.

Workflow tools are not generally considered emerging technology, but the newer versions, called robotic process automation (RPA), which work without human intervention, are viewed as emerging technology. RPA software is programmed to perform routine and repetitive transactions based on a rule-based engine, essentially operating as a virtual workforce that improves the speed and accuracy of the work. The software, or bot, replicates human execution of tasks via existing user interfaces: it captures and interprets existing applications, manipulates data, triggers responses and communicates with other systems. It can also be applied to existing applications without changing the current IT landscape. Organizations using RPA often apply these applications to administrative tasks in onboarding, payroll and benefits to allow HR administrators to manage more complex work in these areas.

Another version of these types of tools that are used to improve business workflows and help get work done in business environments are augmented or virtual reality tools. Augmented reality is a technology that superimposes a computer-generated image on a user's view of the real world, providing a composite or enhanced view of the world. Virtual reality is a computer-generated simulation of a three-dimensional image or environment that can be interacted with in a seemingly real or physical way. In both cases these tools are used to help end-users understand an environment, navigate a process or instruct a computer to complete work that they may not be able to reach physically. Examples of this are extensive and include the British Army using virtual reality for initial training of the Royal Tank Regiment, allowing soldiers to become fully immersed in a training scenario and gain real-time feedback.[2] More subtle examples can simply be the use of a digital adoption platform, such as WalkMe or Whatfix, in which end-users are given hints and guidance on how to use a particular software program, including simulated walk-throughs and help functionality that enhance the use of that software.

Intelligent platforms

Intelligent platforms is a broad way of describing an organization's combined data, insights, algorithms and machine learning technology that is linked together either on a single data environment or through levels of integration. On the absolute edges of the current emerging technology space is the understanding that we are moving ever closer to intelligent platforms that will provide not only data and insights but enterprise recommendations as well.

The far-reaching future of workplace technology is not just being designed to inform our decisions and simplify our activities; it is being designed to capture, catalogue, connect, rank and rate the data in ways that will actually provide context and intelligent guidance. These futuristic concepts are not as far away as we may think – like any intelligent entity, intelligent platforms need time to mature and grow. Currently being educated by today's existing business, consumer and social media data and practices, these platforms are in their toddler stage, just taking their first steps. Currently we are maintaining multiple intelligent platforms, but like the human brain, eventually we will need a holistic intelligent platform where data is housed and accessed by multiple applications inside our organization. A future guided by intelligent technology can seem a bit unnerving, and this is not helped by images from Hollywood or our own recent experience with social media algorithms, but every risk also has a possible upside. Like all technology, the future lies in the hands of those who are building it today, and that is us.

We are creating the building blocks for intelligent platforms – with every transaction, workflow and decision we enter into a system, we are creating the future. Every intelligent platform requires immense amounts of historical and current data to train and test. Although it can be tempting to buy into the vendor hype that you can leapfrog over these data requirements, just imagine your smart phone voice-activated digital assistant trying to explain the multiple variations of your onboarding process to your CEO. If that image is disturbing, think about how the intelligent platform feeding your HR applications will need both data and several layers of context before it becomes a valuable member of an HR Technology ecosystem.

To understand tomorrow's intelligent platform, you must first understand the tools in use today that will eventually become the building blocks of this future environment.

BENCHMARKING DATABASES

Benchmarking, a comparison exercise that organizations undertake against competitors or peers, uses a data set obtained from systems, interviews, surveys or simple observation by an entity that chooses to keep that information. One of the key benefits of using multi-tenant cloud technologies is that, with permission, vendors have the ability to aggregate their client data for more accurate and broader benchmarking efforts in many areas. This may include metrics, activities, usage data or key practices.

One of the current challenges for large enterprise benchmarking efforts is that only categorized and comparable data can be used for analysis, removing the ability to analyze unstructured data such as written comments, notes or even uncategorized fields. Large, contextualized benchmarking databases with data that spans multiple timelines are part of the structured data required for training and validation of effective intelligent platforms of the future.

PREDICTIVE AND PRESCRIPTIVE ANALYTICS

Predictive analytics is a branch of advanced analysis that extrapolates future events based on existing data sets. This advanced process uses multiple techniques, including data mining, predictive modelling and statistical algorithms to assess future possibilities. Organizations wishing to use predictive analytics face a number of challenges, including data quality, data volume and data bias, any one of which could derail a predictive analytics model.

Prescriptive analytics takes predictive outcomes and uses further calculation to place context and judgement on these outcomes and then provides a recommendation on a course of action based on the data. Predictive and prescriptive analytics are an iterative science with models that must be adjusted frequently to achieve accurate and actionable insights.

MACHINE LEARNING

Machine learning is a specific type of system algorithm that gives computers the ability to change their own parameters, based on changing data and inputs, to either take action or provide data. The endgame of machine learning is to develop technology that can grow and teach itself continually as data inputs are received. For the HR space, we see organizations investing in machine learning for recruiting, performance management, health and wellness programmes and operations-specific requirements. Much of what is currently being called artificial intelligence or intelligent systems in HR Technology environments today are early forms of machine learning.

NATURAL LANGUAGE PROCESSING (NLP)

Natural language processing is a branch of computer science and linguistics that uses computer-based methods to analyze language in text and speech. It is literally the study of how humans communicate via spoken and written formats. NLP is already embedded in almost every technology designed and built in the last 10 years – think your search engines, spam filters, text messaging, digital assistants – but we are still searching for the holy grail in this technology. Humans are complex entities, with lots of different languages, dialects, idioms and context that are important in our conversations.

Current NLP tools are facing real scrutiny for being developed mostly for English-speaking environments and serving up biased responses, due to biased training data that impacts important language analysis concerning people of colour, females or other underrepresented populations. It is important to understand these issues and acknowledge the inequities they might cause in your HR and business environments, particularly as the use of NLP continues to expand the data sets it is being asked to analyze, such as market data and sentiment.

SENTIMENT ANALYSIS

Sentiment analysis, sometimes referred to as opinion mining, is the use of natural language processing tools and various forms of text-based analysis tools to determine attitudes, perspectives and opinions in large data sets. These tools often analyze unstructured data required for predictive analytics over time and provide richer context to benchmarking analyses' data and other employee engagement efforts. In the context of sentiment analysis, NLP concerns over bias and data privacy become even more critical as we are ascribing more value to these insights.

BLOCKCHAIN TECHNOLOGIES

Blockchain technology is a data structure that makes it possible to create a digital ledger of transactions and share it among a distributed network of computers. Specifically, it is a growing list of records, called blocks, that are linked using cryptography. Each block contains cryptography, hash/signature (of previous block), timestamp and transaction data.

By design, a blockchain is resistant to modification of the data. It is an open, distributed ledger that can record transactions between two parties in a verifiable and permanent way. Once recorded, the data in any given block cannot be altered retroactively without alteration of all subsequent blocks, which requires consensus of the network majority.

Although this technology is in its very earliest stages, a lot of forward-looking organizations believe blockchain technology will fundamentally change many HR practice areas:

- instant payroll/non-cash payments;
- reference checks;
- certification verification;
- performance ratings;
- job/career history management;
- background checks.

Each of these emerging technology categories has real opportunities to propel our industry forward, and high levels of risk for any organization that does not manage them carefully. Major issues that need to be addressed in any organization currently using or planning to use these emerging technologies include:

- data privacy standards;
- standards on the ethical use of data;
- data security practices;
- data maintenance practices;
- systemic racism and institutional bias;
- ethical system designs.

The history of emerging HR Technology

While HR Technology transformation efforts may seem slow and sometimes painful, in tech terms they have been quite rapid. Within 20 years, the focus of HR Technology applications has shifted from administrative tools to end-user engagement platforms; over the last 10 years, cloud has gone from a concept to a reality, with 70 per cent of organizations deploying at least one cloud-based HR application.[3] Non-HR business applications are moving just as fast, with the number of organizations deploying applications in the cloud doubling in the last four years.

There are numerous models and explanations put forth by the technology pundits around how a technology moves from an idea to emerging technology, to hyper-growth technology and then to massive adoption. Gartner has its 'Technology Hype Cycle', which proposes that every new technology goes through an evolution period that runs from innovation trigger to the trough of disillusionment and finally to the plateau of productivity.[4] Moore's law is an observation that turned into a self-fulfilling prophecy, that the density of an integrated circuit would double every two years. An industry focused on constant growth and change took this observation as fact and used it to plan production and research cycles for almost every other hardware-based technology advancement since his prediction in 1975. Mary Meeker is a venture capitalist and former Wall Street securities analyst, who every year since 1995 has been producing one of the most highly anticipated internet trends reports for technology investors. Her mammoth annual report is filled with facts and figures from around the globe that she uses to make judgement calls on which technology trends will be hot for the next few years.[5] No matter the model, philosophy or pundit you follow to inform your emerging HR Technology thinking, the important thing is to ensure you are spending time thinking about it.

The real history of emerging technology inside an organization is not found in the constant change and rush to buy the newest products but rather in the strategy an organization takes towards innovation, change management, and technology selection and purchases. These factors will give you a much better understanding of how your current HR Technology environment came to be in existence and the impact that will have on available data, security and integration points.

Why you need to care

When we look beyond the immediate future of today's technology, it is easy to feel as though we are stepping into the next science-fiction novel as we discuss driverless cars, household appliances that run our lives, and shopping environments that know more about us than our own parents know. The reality is that the future is now, and the technology around us is changing daily.

In the earliest days of HR Technology adoption, research clearly showed there was a tight connection between investing in HR Technology and organizations achieving higher levels of efficiency and better business outcomes. As technology becomes more commonly adopted in any area, the higher levels of value achieved by early adopters start to decrease, and ultimately not having the technology begins to cost an organization. Similarly, organizations will need to decide at what point the benefits outweigh the risk in adopting the technologies we have covered in this chapter. Eventually every company takes a step into the future if it is to survive. As an HR or IT professional, being prepared and ready for that step makes you more valuable to your organization and offers more options if your role is impacted by the new technology.

Emerging technologies are always in the early stages of development and are often simply tools or partial applications that may cause you frustration and confusion. Nevertheless, it is important to monitor their adoption rates because many will have an impact on the future of HR applications and the move to intelligent HR systems that will be part of your future.

It is also helpful to keep in mind that in this emerging generation of intelligent systems, the technology itself becomes less important than how it is connected to the broader work environment, how information is captured, shared and ultimately categorized for future learning algorithms. Today's artificial intelligence (AI) or learning technology is still in its infancy, like a young child who can understand patterns but has only limited judgement. The technology is exposed only to the information provided by its environment, which means it develops biases, makes poor judgement calls and misinterprets human behaviour to the same extent as we do, but 100 times faster. Intelligent systems also analyze and read more data than a human being could comprehend when making decisions and has the potential to improve our lives exponentially when applied to health, workforce and economic challenges.

Looking forward, technology and industry trends will continue to change, but one theme stands out as a constant thread for the foreseeable future: how organizations consume, manage and leverage data makes a vast difference in their ability to prepare for tomorrow. An organization's strategy and approach to data management are tightly connected to the outcomes an organization can achieve from its technology investments.

Another reason to stay informed on the trends in emerging technologies is to understand the audience you are serving as an HR and IT professional. Consumerization of technology is not a new concept; it's been around since the evolution of the app generation. It is fairly new to HR Technology environments, and HR decision makers need to acknowledge that end-users are accustomed to engaging and intuitive personal technology, and they expect no less from their organizations' enterprise systems.

Looking back with awe and amazement at the technical accomplishments of this industry, we are ever mindful that HR still exists as a very personal experience for the individual. On the corporate side, HR Technology provides the vehicle through which organizations streamline processes, effectively allocate resources and innovate within their HR function. For the workforce, our personal lives have become more integrated with our work lives, illustrating the point that when HR Technology works at its best, it provides the framework through which balance can be achieved for everyone. Looking forward, HR Technology may be facing its greatest challenge yet: the future will not be judged by cost savings and ease of use but rather by value creation and workforce experiences. In this new world, transparency will be expected and yet trust is paramount – and the responsibility for enterprise communications may fall to tomorrow's HR Technology environments.

The future of technology is not something to hide from or fear but rather to walk into with eyes open, clearly evaluating the risks, rewards, limitations and possibilities inherent in any technology adoption.

HANDS-ON ACTIVITIES

- Ask your HRIT or IT leader to rank your organization's comfort level with emerging technology risk on a scale of 1–5 (1 being very risk averse and 5 being open to experimentation).

- Discuss with your HRIT or IT leader whether they believe they are using any emerging technologies in these categories:

  o monitoring technologies

  o communication technologies

  o workflow and augmentation tools

  o intelligent platforms

- Is your organization using any HR application that leverages these intelligent technologies? If so, in what platforms?

- Select one HR application that includes one of these emerging tools and discuss with your HR, HRIT or IT leader whether these questions can be answered:

  o Who is liable for decisions recommended by the application?

  o Can we change the underlying data scheme or training data used to inform the algorithm? If not, why?

  o What happens to the data if we decide to turn off the application?

  o How often do we audit or test the data or recommendations it provides against other non-computer-generated methods of decision making?

Endnotes

1   Smith, Duncan (2011) The Forgotten Inventor of the Motor Car, *Vienna Review,* https://www.theviennareview.at/archives/2011/the-forgotten-inventor-of-the-motor-car (archived at https://perma.cc/7PJP-DCYN)

2   British Army (2019) Virtual reality training, *YouTube* www.youtube.com/watch?v=lOxBOPWej3k&feature=emb_logo (archived at https://perma.cc/7PJP-DCYN)

3   Sapient Insights, 2020–2021 HR Systems Survey White Paper, 23rd Annual Edition

4   Gartner (2020) Gartner Hype Cycle, www.gartner.com/en/research/methodologies/gartner-hype-cycle (archived at https://perma.cc/243J-DBLU)

5   Rooney, K (2019) Mary Meeker just published her highly anticipated internet trends report – read it here, *CNBC*, 11 June, www.cnbc.com/2019/06/11/mary-meeker-just-published-her-highly-anticipated-internet-trends-report-read-it-here.html (archived at https://perma.cc/2V6W-24AT)

11

HR Technology as an environment

Pulling it all together

A total HR Technology environment is much like the community we discussed in the preface – with infrastructure, communications, major buildings and minor but relevant stores that provide resources for the entire community.

One way to look at an HR Technology environment is by visualizing how all the pieces fit together and interact. The HR systems adoption blueprint (Figure 11.1) can be viewed as a series of containers, each connected through interrelated elements. This works best when considering the essential connection points of an entire HR systems environment – those connection points are as important as individual applications.

Level one: strategy, culture, data governance

Three foundational elements are at the centre of the HR systems adoption blueprint:

- strategy;
- culture;
- data governance.

HR applications impact all aspects of an organization's operations, are likely to be used by nearly every employee, and possibly extend to vendors and contractors. Taking the time to define the outcomes you

FIGURE 11.1   The HR systems adoption blueprint

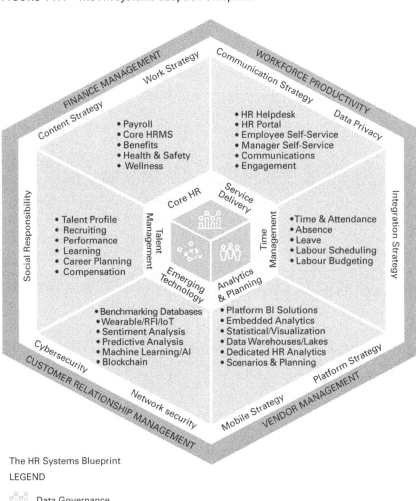

The HR Systems Blueprint
LEGEND

 Data Governance

 Strategy

 Culture

▨ Guiding Principles

▨ HR System Applications

▨ Enterprise Standards

▨ Enterprise Work Applications

expect from your HR systems implementation, in terms of your enterprise strategy, always pays off. Organizations that consider the long-term impact of systems on their mission, goals and workforce are more likely to select applications that grow with them and respond to what makes their organization unique.

Organizations often focus solely on specific functionality desired from HR Technology and supporting processes but may overlook how that functionality will actually work within their unique culture. Technology is of little value if it is not used – it must fit within the context of how an organization operates and how decisions are made to optimize the investment.

The footprint of workforce data goes beyond business applications, it extends into social networks, mingles with environmental tools and overlaps with personal profiles. Data governance is a major factor in the design of your HR Technology environment, as it defines how you capture, access, use, protect and eventually purge necessary data. HR Technology should help you achieve the most value from your workforce data while ensuring adherence to ethical and legal standards.

Level two: HR application environments – technology at work

Within each primary HR system category there are numerous HR applications designed to address the various strategic, cultural and procedural requirements requested by buyers. Surrounding the foundational elements are six primary categories of enterprise HR system applications:

• core HR management;
• service delivery;
• time management;
• talent management;
• analytics and planning;
• emerging technology.

CORE HR APPLICATIONS: GETTING THE BASICS RIGHT

The HR systems journey starts by deploying core HR applications, initially in the form of a payroll solution. Payroll solutions are often implemented with an HRMS, but payroll systems can be stand-alone, leveraging the basic data-capturing capabilities in place of an HRMS until their needs expand. For most organizations, the HRMS sits at the heart of their HR and workforce data management needs, sharing data across HR applications.

As organizations grow and become more complex, an HRMS becomes necessary to manage the regulatory and data management requirements of their enterprise workforce; increasingly, even smaller organizations find it necessary to implement an HRMS with solid effective dating capabilities. Benefits applications are the most diverse HR application area, covering pension and retirement plans, stock options, healthcare, wellness benefits and voluntary/flexible benefits. The adoption of benefits applications is highly dependent on regional HR standards. In the US, most organizations have adopted a benefits application, primarily to manage corporate sponsored healthcare. In regions where healthcare is government-sponsored, such as Europe or Asia-Pacific countries, we see fewer adoptions.

Health and safety was once an HR application used primarily in manufacturing or utility environments, but today the necessity for these applications has grown exponentially with increases in environmental issues, health crises and shifting regional compliance requirements. An application designed to help organizations manage employee health, reduce safety risks and maintain operational continuity during crisis events has become a critical tool for HR. We are just starting to assess these areas and will have more data on these applications next year.

Organizations with a history of regional expansion, or mergers and acquisitions, often have multiple core HR applications in use to meet the needs of their various workforces and regional markets. It is not uncommon for the integration of these multiple systems to become the focus of consolidation efforts to achieve better workforce information sharing, help drive efficiencies and reduce costs within the organization.

HR SERVICE DELIVERY APPLICATIONS: USER EXPERIENCE

When core HR applications are adopted, there is naturally some level of administrative efficiency achieved for an HR function. However, as organizations increase in size and complexity, they also need to consider employee-facing HR applications, including:

- employee and manager HR self-service;
- employee HR portal;
- HR content and document management;
- HR communications and feedback;
- employee helpdesk/case management.

These are all critical data-collection and information-sharing tools that are tightly connected to talent, HR and even business outcomes. Organizations that invest in at least one service delivery application often see higher levels of employee engagement and system adoption, along with increased HR efficiencies. These applications are significantly influenced by consumer trends, creating employee expectations for emerging technologies across these application areas.

TIME AND TALENT MANAGEMENT: BUSINESS APPLICATIONS

Time management and talent management application adoption tightly connects with an organization's business needs, although the initial adoption of these applications may be in response to a specific operational request. Although these two areas may seem separate in their focus, they work hand in hand for organizations balancing business needs with employee aspirations, and are also tightly connected to employee culture and engagement.

Time management applications, sometimes referred to as workforce management applications, provide operational oversight to areas such as:

- time and attendance;
- absence management;
- leave management;

- labour scheduling;
- labour budgeting.

These applications are critical for organizations carefully managing the hours worked, location and schedules for large employee populations.

Talent management applications provide operational oversight for areas such as:

- recruiting/talent acquisition;
- onboarding/mobility;
- performance management;
- learning and development;
- compensation management;
- employee profile/competencies/skills;
- succession and career management.

Many of these requirements can be handled manually by smaller organizations, but they quickly become system priorities for those organizations managing large workforces, multiple projects or seeing fast growth.

ANALYTICS AND PLANNING: INCREASING VALUE

Adoption of the core HR, service delivery, time management and talent management applications provides an organization with clear benefits in the areas of HR efficiency and process management. However, the real value of these systems is realized in data analysis to provide people analytics and planning, also referred to as HR business intelligence (HR BI). Applications and tools that support analytics and planning efforts help organizations to capture, store, govern, analyze, report and share past, present and future workforce information. The applications may also provide statistical analysis and proprietary algorithms that can deliver insights, recommendations, predictions, scenarios and forecasts to be used for decision-making and workforce-planning purposes. These applications can be focused solely on HR efforts or share space with other enterprise applications, providing the opportunity to cross-analyze data from both inside and outside the organization.

The category of analytics and planning applications is still in its infancy; it currently exists as a combination of embedded analytics packages that are part of other HR applications, for which 32 per cent of organizations pay extra fees, and several stand-alone platforms and tools, including Microsoft Excel.

EMERGING TECHNOLOGY APPLICATIONS: LOOKING TO THE FUTURE

Emerging technologies are in the early stages of development and are often simply tools or partial applications. Nevertheless, it is important to monitor their adoption rates because many will have an impact on the future of HR applications and the move to intelligent HR systems. The major categories in this area include:

- monitoring technologies;
- communication technologies;
- workflow and augmentation;
- intelligent platforms.

These applications and tools are both opportunities and risks, and should be evaluated with that in mind. Organizations that choose to invest in emerging technologies should think in terms of moving fast, but assessing often. Organizations should watch for any gaps in safety, security or financial risks, ethical concerns or lack of follow-through on the part of the technology as well as the vendor providing it.

Level three: enterprise standards – the great connectors

Surrounding the six categories of HR systems applications in the blueprint is a layer of critical enterprise standards that play a major role in the success or failure of application investments. The most critical standards include:

- social responsibility;
- content strategy;
- work strategy;
- communication strategy;
- data privacy;
- integration strategy;

- platform strategy;
- mobile strategy;
- network security;
- cybersecurity.

Connecting HR systems to enterprise standards allows organizations to embed HR solutions seamlessly and safely into everyday work environments and share data across multiple system environments. Working within these standards provides a level of context, guidance and ethical frameworks for HR applications that is critical as we move forward into a future of intelligent platforms.

Enterprise work applications: workscapes

HR technologies coexist in a larger environment represented by the outer rim of our blueprint, which includes enterprise business applications such as finance management, workforce productivity applications (Microsoft, Google, project management, etc), customer relationship management and vendor management. Depending on the organization's industry and the type of work it actually does, there could be many more enterprise applications that fit into this category.

These solutions are where work occurs daily and where an abundance of additional data is captured, stored and used repeatedly for business decisions. HR and HRIT have an important role in staying on top of how these applications are gathering and using employee data and ensuring all government and ethical standards are being followed. Creating a clear picture of these applications, how security is managed and how HR needs to connect, communicate and share data with these applications is critical to achieving outcomes desired by leaders.

Continuous change management: achieving outcomes

'Build it and they will come' is a nice plot for a movie, but it rarely works when investing in enterprise-level technology. To achieve high levels of adoption, and therefore real outcomes, when investing in HR Technology, organizations need to adopt a model of continuous

FIGURE 11.2   Continuous change management model

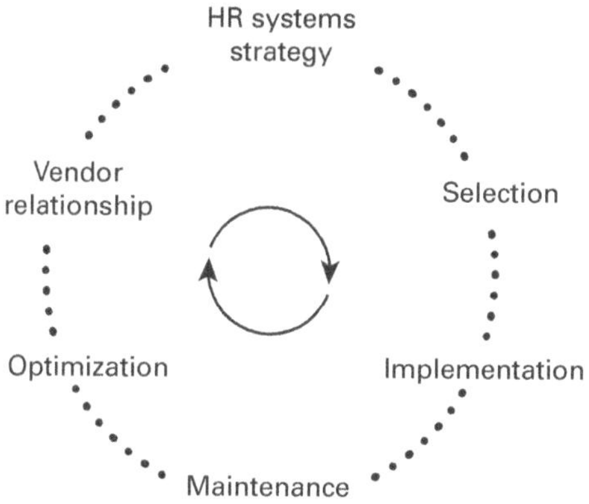

change management, as seen in Figure 11.2. The final component of our blueprint represents the organization's change management approach, including standards for developing an HR systems strategy and managing the selection, implementation, maintenance optimization and vendor relationships for the entire HR systems environment. A continuous change management model for HR systems environments consistently aligns with better talent, HR and business outcomes. Employing a continuous change management approach has resulted in 21 per cent higher average outcomes over the last five years in research.[1]

Whether change is driven internally by strategic initiatives or in reaction to external forces as experienced by many organizations during the global health crisis, all change impacts people, culture, procedures, technology and available data. Change management efforts are designed to assess the impact of change, drive that change and ultimately achieve a sustainable outcome.

There are generally four types of system change management approaches in most organizations today:

- **Culture of change management** – continuous assessment of all change events, with ongoing governance, communication, feedback mechanisms and measurement to ensure change goals are being achieved and creating positive outcomes over time.

- **Project-based change management** – key projects that meet size, budget or breadth of stakeholder criteria receive standard project-based change efforts that include short-term governance, communication and measurement.

- **Sporadic change management** – done on an ad hoc basis, no criteria, no standard approach to change efforts.

- **No change management** – not in the budget or resource plans, no change management efforts conducted.

Doing something is generally better than doing nothing, but that is not always the case with change management. Project-based change management practices are based on the idea that all projects have a beginning, middle and end, with consistent goals determined at the beginning of the process and achieved at the completion of the project.

In reality, goals shift frequently and key performance indicators (KPIs) adjust to expected outcomes. Organizations should be prepared to continue some level of ongoing change management after the 'go-live' event of major projects to ensure the KPIs are achieved and the change is fulfilled. It is not uncommon in project-based change management for user adoption to decline post-implementation when change management resources are redeployed to the next project. Large financial investments in project-based change initiatives that lack support for continuous change management often achieve similar long-term outcomes as in those organizations that practise no change management. In other words, the change is less important than the approach you take to making that change.

Constant change is simply a part of our everyday lives and waiting for things to 'get back to normal' disregards the importance of the changes we experience. Real change necessitates a shift away from thinking of change management as a once-and done initiative to the creation of an adaptable organization with the skills and resources needed to support continuous change management.

A continuous change management model provides a basis for our HR system decision making; every change impacts the people, culture, processes, other systems and eventually the data in your organization. Every change drives an outcome, and ensuring a positive outcome – increased adoption, engagement, flow of data or workforce readiness – requires mindful management. With this lens, the processes we often regard as separate work or initiatives are in fact connected under the umbrella of continuous change management. When viewed holistically, change management can include all of the following efforts:

- HR systems strategy;
- selection management;
- implementation management;
- maintenance and optimization;
- vendor relationship management.

The HR systems strategy

Creating an HR Technology environment that helps us achieve our outcomes requires careful planning and constant evaluation. The complex and intelligent platforms that make up today's HR systems environments are filled with both potential and risk for an organization. The first step in the process is to understand your organizational and HR strategies.

Within the HR function, chief Human Resources officers (CHROs) often struggle to balance the multiple positions they are asked to hold in an organization, from employee advocate and business leader to keeper of the organizational culture. CHROs have the difficult task of prioritizing HR resource investments to achieve the greatest outcomes, and historically those outcomes were focused on processes and regulations. Without technology and data, HR's limited resources were needed to reduce regulatory risk and, as much as possible, standardize employee expectations through policies.

As technology helps to create HR efficiencies and gathers data that allows us to recognize employees as individuals, CHROs are now able to shift their leadership and ultimately the perception of HR from a cost centre to a value creator. Value comes in the form of definable outcomes necessary to achieve organizational goals. An outcome-focused approach to HR simply shifts the focus from reaction, policy and processes to a discernable vision of the future. Outcomes are definable, measurable expectations for what the customer, employee and stakeholders achieve from the work of your organization.

Our approach to HR has always been a combined response to business needs and societal changes, but this preemptive approach to HR means that financial metrics can be tightly connected to other critical outcomes such as market share, brand, innovation, employee engagement and workforce experiences. Business and organizational outcomes can be achieved in multiple ways. An HR function that understands this can put forth an approach to HR for employees and management that focuses on outcomes. To help the organization make the hard decisions about acknowledging or changing its culture, an HR function needs to hold up a mirror for leaders to see how real organizational priorities are set and decisions are made. To achieve value, an HR function needs to understand the outcomes expected from its stakeholders and break the standard approach to HR, as seen in Figure 11.3.

Once an organization has clearly defined its approach to HR and the outcomes it plans to achieve, it can begin to build out an HR systems strategy. A regularly updated HR systems strategy is reviewed every 12–18 months and should include:

- expected outcomes;
- current state analysis;
- phased road maps;
- key performance indicators;
- change management strategy.

The complex and intelligent platforms that make up an HR systems environment require an enterprise HR systems strategy to guide and inform the flow of data and corresponding business decisions. The value of an enterprise HR systems strategy that is regularly reviewed can be seen in multiple areas, including consistent messaging, clearly defined business outcomes and an improved perception of the overall HR function.

FIGURE 11.3   Shifting from transactional to outcome-focused human resources

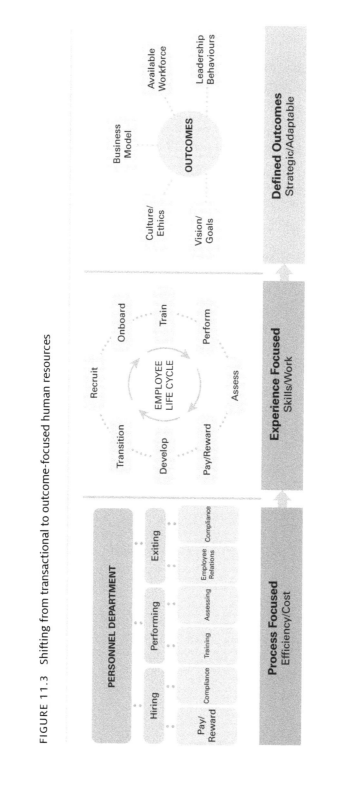

Elements of an enterprise HR systems strategy

Most organizations report that their enterprise HR systems strategies are reviewed annually, with minor adjustments made each year. Every organization has a unique approach to building its HR systems strategies, but the most often reported elements of a regularly updated HR systems strategy include those shown in the table.

TABLE 11.1 HR systems strategy elements

Business /Mission Drivers	Enterprise documentation of the prioritized business outcomes and required talent and HR outcomes to achieve them. Alignment of Enterprise HCM system gaps that impact those outcomes.
Culture, Scale, and Scope	Careful account of the organization's cultural environment including its approach to enterprise decision making. A detailed understanding of the organization's workforce makeup, locations, and technology access.
Current State Blueprint	A catalog of the organization's current Enterprise HCM systems environment, including applications in use, vendor relationship details, and environmental factors such as privacy, integrations, infrastructure models, etc
Benchmarking Analysis	Data or analyses of how the organization's current state compares to peer organizations in culture, size, industry, or complexity
Gap Analysis & Necessary Changes	Gap analysis and recommended changes based on business, talent, and HR outcomes as well as peer benchmarking analysis.
Future State Blueprint	A clear vision of the future state of the Enterprise HCM systems environment, including adoption expectations, user experience factors, and expected business outcomes
Phased Roadmaps	Timelines, responsibilities, communication plans, and Key Performance Indicators (KPIs) associated with any approved application changes or updates.
Governance and Change Management	Identified decision makers, ownership models, and guidelines for making ongoing decisions on Enterprise HCM system environments, data management, and privacy issues. Ongoing change management and adoption efforts.
Expenditures and Budgets	Past expenditures and future budgets for Enterprise HCM system environments
Resources and Outsourcing	Careful account of both internal and external resources, as well as outsourcing agreements that support the Enterprise HCM systems environments.

Our changing workforce and business environments should not be a cause for alarm, unless an organization is fixed on the notion that every employee should be treated the same. In this new world we are entering, every employee and candidate should be treated with respect, and their individuality celebrated and acknowledged. Candidate selections need to be based on clearly defined criteria and actual data, and employee and employer relationships should be based on a clear understanding of how information will be used to make decisions and support business goals as well as an employee's personal goals. Technology should be an enabler in our goal to meet the needs of our changing workforce, specifically providing solutions that not only capture data but provide context and insight, along with personalized experiences tailored to individual needs and preferences. None of this is possible without a solid HR systems strategy.

The journey continues – keep learning

This book has been written specifically with the information that I wish someone had shared with me when I started my HR Technology journey and hopefully it will give you a step up in your own journey. As lengthy and detailed as this book has been, it is truly just the tip of the iceberg when it comes to the HR Technology market, and my fervent hope is that this has piqued your interest and will encourage you to keep learning.

Critical topics that I recommend you look into along your journey include:

- HR systems professionals: roles, responsibilities and domains;
- building an HR Technology business case;
- developing an HR systems strategy;
- integrations and system interrelationships;
- business process improvement efforts;
- HR system selection, implementation and upgrades;
- HR system maintenance and data management;

- HR system business continuity plans;
- HR systems vendor relationship management;
- HR data privacy, ethics and standards.

Many books cover these topics, as do formal education programmes, but I also recommend building a network of colleagues to help you on your journey. There are great associations like the International Association for Human Resource Information Management (IHRIM), with a focus on the HR Technology profession.[2] Other general HR associations like the Chartered Institute of Personnel and Development (CIPD) and the Society for Human Resource Management (SHRM), both global organizations, offer networking opportunities and education on technology in the HR space.

In an environment of endless transition, the best leaders understand that change is a constant variable that needs to be built into each decision put before them. My role as a researcher gives me the opportunity to speak with business leaders around the globe – and whether or not it is explicitly stated, every conversation includes the desire to manage the pace of change to allow for better decision making. In reality, HR and IT business leaders must adapt and grow, putting in place a continuous improvement model that takes into consideration this variable of constant change. HR systems strategies require flexibility and a clear understanding of how an organization expects the workforce to support its unique organizational goals. Change is simply part of the ongoing equation of work.

HANDS-ON ACTIVITIES

- Ask your HRIT or IT leaders whether your organization has or is developing an enterprise HR systems strategy.
  - If yes, when was it last updated and who owns the maintenance?
- Discuss with your HRIT or IT leader which of these categories of change management they believe the organization subscribes to:
  - **Culture of change management**: continuous assessment of all change events, with ongoing governance, communication, feedback

mechanisms and measurement to ensure change goals are being achieved and creating positive outcomes over time.

○ **Project-based change management**: key projects that meet size, budget or breadth of stakeholder criteria receive standard project-based change efforts that include short-term governance, communication and measurement.

○ **Sporadic change management**: done on an ad hoc basis, no criteria, no standard approach to change efforts.

○ **No change management**: not in the budget or resource plans, no change management efforts conducted.

• Sign up and attend a free HR Technology webinar at IHRIM, SHRM or CIPD.

• Use LinkedIn to connect with at least three colleagues outside your organization who have HR Technology responsibilities.

THE HUMAN SIDE OF HR TECHNOLOGY ENVIRONMENTS: PULLING IT ALL TOGETHER GLOBALLY

'Don't underestimate the time you'll need to win hearts and minds.'

A truly global outlook is essential when introducing a centralized HR system for large multi-national organizations, but it is the perspective that is often missed the most when organizations rush to roll out new technology and processes. Balancing a global approach with local sensibilities is no easy task, but one that pays off when trying to gain buy-in across multiple geographies.

In 2016, FedEx decided that it needed to review its payroll setup and time and attendance. With 'extremely localized staff' in 220 countries, many were resistant to change. The current payroll setup was spread over 68 different providers and 100 teams worldwide. FedEx knew there needed to be a change, requiring a new way of thinking about Payroll and Time. With 490,000 employees, the shift from a localized approach to a more global one was essential. When starting on this project, FedEx and their global Payroll vendor, ADP, came together in the Netherlands and 'locked themselves in a room for two weeks to conduct a harmonization effort.

Although the project manager leading the consolidation effort wanted to be very hands on and take the pressure off local payroll teams busy with the business of paying employees, she quickly realized that the local teams needed to be involved in the process. Their involvement would help the organization appreciate the cultural differences in each country and ensure the teams felt their perspectives were considered. Adapting the communications style was critical to achieving successful change.

If your global growth is hindered because you don't have a good view of your people data that is a problem that needs addressed immediately. FedEx can now report on its global employees' payroll information inside the ADP dashboard, allowing the team to deliver global payroll that calculates precisely what they set out to do. No project succeeds without adoption, and the change management efforts are the real hero in most implementation stories, including this one.[3]

Endnotes

1   Sapient Insights, 2020–2021 HR Systems Survey White Paper, 23rd Annual Edition
2   International Association for Human Resource Information Management, Vision, purpose and values, https://ihrim.org/about/vision-purpose-and-values/ (archived at https://perma.cc/3MJ8-KNUK)
3   https://rethink.adp.com/wp-content/uploads/2020/04/ADP_ReThink_ Guide_2020.pdf

INDEX

182   INDEX

continuous change management 170–73
change management approaches
culture of change management 171
no change management 172
project-based change
management 172
sporadic change management 172
continuous change management
model 171
drivers of change 171
key performance indicators (KPIs) 172
core HR administration applications 5,
47–61, 49
activities to assess 58–59
adoption of 50, 50
application turnover 58
application types
benefits administration 53, 53, 54,
166
health and safety 166
Human Resources management
system (HRMS) 52, 166
payroll and tax
administration 50–52, 53, 54,
56, 166
case studies 60–61
data, usefulness of 57–58
getting the basics right 166
history of 54–56
effective dating 54–55
global working, challenges of 55–56
need for accuracy 57
outsourcing of 53–54
Cornerstone OnDemand 21, 108–09
Reporting and Analytics 130
COVID-19 pandemic 24–26, 26, 32,
112, 139
absence and leave management
applications 87, 88
as a driver of change 171
top HR initiatives in 2020 25
crowdsourcing 33
Curie, Marie 147
CyberU 208–09

data capture
biometric monitoring 151
enterprise work applications 170
environmental monitoring 151
surveys and interviews 150
video, audio and desktop
monitoring 150–51
wearables 150

data cleansing 129, 133
data governance 4, 44, 45, 113, 163, 165
data lakes 130
data management and manipulation
tools 130
data privacy 30, 43, 52, 113, 157, 169, 178
and COVID-19 26
and emerging technologies 72, 158
and monitoring devices 151
and talent management applications 99,
100, 101, 102, 104, 105
and time management applications 88
data security 30, 52, 113
data breach reporting 133
and emerging technologies 72, 158, 159
personal identifiable information 133
responsibility for 43, 43, 44, 45
data sharing tools 130
data visualization tools 129, 130
data warehouses 130
Da Vinci, Leonardo 147
Dayforce 23
Dell 76–77
acquisition of EMC 76
descriptive analytics 122, 124
desktop monitoring 150–51
diagnostic analytics 124
digital assistants 67, 71–72, 155
Docent 21
Douyin see TikTok

Edison, Thomas 147
effective dating 54–55
Electronic Privacy Information Centre
(EPIC) 114
embedded analytics 129–30
EMC 76
emerging HR Technology 5, 143–62, 146,
169
activities to assess 161–62
application types
communication technologies 151–53
intelligent platforms 154–55
monitoring technologies 149–51
workflow and automation
tools 153–54
defining 145
history of 158–59
innovation 145, 147–49
'employee experience platforms' 71
employee helpdesk and case
management 68–69
employee self-service (ESS) 30, 35, 68, 85

EU Representative (GPSR)

Authorised Rep Compliance Ltd, Ground Floor, 71 Lower Baggot Street, Dublin, D02 P593, Ireland

www.arccompliance.com

www.ingramcontent.com/pod-product-compliance
Lightning Source LLC
Chambersburg PA
CBHW050257200525
26983CB00016B/984